MW01590855

SORROW TO EVERLASTING JOY

By Jeannette Musselman

PRESS

ACKNOWLEDGEMENTS
AND BOOK REVIEWS

I wish to express my appreciation to:

Pastor Dale Hoch for reading through my manuscript, for his spiritual guidance and many helpful comments. (Please see his review on the back cover.)

Solvejg Cole and Carrie Waterman for reading my manuscript and encouraging me to publish it. (Please see their reviews below.)

Thank you very much. You were all a tremendous help and inspiration to me during this process.

In reading this book, I grew in my walk with Jesus in leaps and bounds. There were verses in the Bible which I simply could not grasp the meaning of until I read this book. I have read this book several times as I wanted to keep the truths that are presented fresh in my mind. I am applying the truths that I now understand to my everyday life. Oh my, what a joy to finally get it! There are many people who need to grab hold of the truths in this book as it will bring freedom to them and a transformed life. Solvejg Cole

If you have any doubts about who you are in Christ and how much the Lord loves you, then this is the book to read. This book is a guide for all who want to learn of God's love for them and how to live in His love. The reader will discover the difference between law and grace. It shows how we can live in grace and truth in our relationship with Jesus. This is an inspiring and informative book with scriptural references and explanations. For those who want to learn and grow in all that God has for you, this is an amazing read. Carrie Waterman

INDEX

Jesus Came To Set You Free

As you begin to read this Book, please realize that you cannot set yourself free from sorrow or any other negative emotion but God can and He will if you let Him. Please read this Book with the understanding that you are totally dependent upon God's grace to set you free, not your performance. Grace is the undeserved, unmerited, unearned favor of God. We cannot earn, merit or deserve God's grace. Grace is a free gift to us from Jesus when we believe in Him with our hearts as our Savior and our Lord.

Would you pray the following prayer:

Prayer: Father, in Jesus' Name, thank You that You accept me just the way I am. I come to You, Jesus, just the way I am and I lay myself and all sorrow, sadness, grief, depression, anger, loneliness, etc. at Your feet. I need Your help. I need Your grace. Please help me to receive the healing that Jesus suffered to give to me and help me to receive revelation as I read this Book. Please set me free by the truth. Help me to read this Book in its entirety with the understanding that Your grace is a free gift and help me to **receive** the full benefit of what You have for me. Help me to know that I cannot set myself free but You can and You will do it. Help me to understand that my part is to believe and receive and You will do the rest. Please help me to receive Your grace and Your gift of righteousness so that I can walk in wholeness.

If you have had depression, sorrow, grief, anger, addictions, etc. for a long time, please allow God's grace to destroy these strongholds as you put the truths in this Book into your heart. Please don't read this Book in one sitting. If you do you will miss so much of what Jesus has for you. You need to read it slowly and think about what you are reading. Let the truths permeate your heart so that you can receive them and benefit from them.

I am using many scriptures throughout this Book so that you can clearly see that it is God's Will for you to have joy in your everyday life. He wants you to enjoy your life and He wants you to enjoy Him. The whole time you read this Book, keep your eyes on Jesus who is the only One that is able to set you free by His grace. So let's begin our journey from sorrow to everlasting joy.

> *"The Spirit of the Sovereign Lord is on me, because the Lord has anointed me to preach good news to the poor. He has sent me to bind up the brokenhearted, to proclaim freedom for the captives and release from darkness for the prisoners, to proclaim the year of the Lord's favor and the day of vengeance of our God, to comfort all who mourn, and provide for those who grieve in Zion – to bestow on them a crown of beauty instead of ashes, the oil of gladness instead of mourning, and a garment of praise instead of a spirit of despair" (Isaiah 61:1-3a).*

This scripture is talking about Jesus and why He came into this world. He came to set us free by the truth, to heal our hearts, to destroy strongholds in our lives, to provide for us and to give us His grace. He came to comfort us, give us His life and to restore joy to us. Simply speaking He came to make us whole in every area of our lives.

Quite a few years ago, I was in a healing line. I asked the Holy Spirit what I should ask for when it was my turn to be prayed for. There were so many things I needed. I will never forget what the Holy Spirit said to me. He said to ask for "wholeness". I knew it was the Holy Spirit as I had never thought about asking for that before. In fact, when I told the Pastor what I wanted to be prayed for, I could see by the look on his face that he had never had anyone ask him for that. It is God's Will to bring wholeness to each one of His children, without exception.

Now let's continue to look at Isaiah 61 in verse 7. "Instead of their shame my people will receive a double portion, and instead of disgrace they will **rejoice** in their inheritance; and so they will inherit a double portion in their land, and **everlasting joy** will be theirs."

God promises us that He will replace our shame and disgrace with a double portion of our inheritance and everlasting (eternal) joy will be ours. Will you receive the double portion of what Jesus has already provided for you as you read about your inheritance throughout this Book? As you read through this Book, you will see some things that you have inherited from Jesus because you belong to Him. In fact, I have dedicated a chapter in this Book on our inheritance in Christ Jesus. When someone dies, the inheritance must be received in order for the heir to benefit from that inheritance. We need to know what our inheritance is, as a child of God, in order to receive it.

In this next scripture reference, David was crying out to the Lord for help. I want you to pay close attention to how God responded to his cry in order to rescue him from his enemies. As you cry out to God, God will respond the same way to you. Know that God does not want you to beg Him for His help as if He is unwilling to help you. When it says that David cried to the Lord, he was not begging the Lord. This scripture refers to the fervency of David's heart to God. David knew that God would help him. God is willing to help you. When you pray, pray knowing that God will help you.

> *"In my distress I called to the Lord; I cried to my God for help. From his temple he heard my voice; my cry came before him, into his ears. The earth trembled and quaked, and the foundations of the mountains shook; they trembled because he was angry. Smoke rose from his nostrils; consuming fire came from his mouth, burning coals blazed out of it. He parted the heavens and came down; dark clouds were under his feet. He mounted the cherubim and flew; he soared on the wings of the wind. He made darkness his covering, his canopy around him – the dark, rain clouds*

of the sky. Out of the brightness of his presence clouds advanced, with hailstones and bolts of lightning. The Lord thundered from heaven; the voice of the Most High resounded. He shot his arrows and scattered the enemies, great bolts of lightning and routed them. The valleys of the sea were exposed and the foundations of the earth laid bare at your rebuke, O Lord, at the blast of breath from your nostrils. He reached down from on high and took hold of me; he drew me out of deep waters. He rescued me from my powerful enemy, from my foes, who were too strong for me. They confronted me in the day of my disaster, but the Lord was my support. He brought me out into a spacious place; he rescued me because he delighted in me" (Psalm 18:6-19).

This is how God responds to us when we cry out to Him in faith. Mark this Psalm in your Bible so that you can refer to it as often as you need to.

Picture Jesus reaching His arm down from heaven towards you and picture yourself grabbing a hold of His hand to pull you up out of that pit of sorrow, sadness, discouragement, etc. and to gently bring you into His Presence. Close your eyes and picture this.

Have you ever thought about Jesus being your Stronghold? We often think of a stronghold in the negative sense only. There are strongholds in our life that need to be destroyed by the truth of God's Word so that we can be free from them. However, I want you to think about Jesus as your Stronghold. He is your strong high tower. He is your refuge. He is your ever present help in times of trouble. The following are a few scriptures that tell us this. As you read them, meditate on them and take a few minutes to thank the Lord that He is your Stronghold, your Refuge, your Fortress, your Deliverer and your Savior.

"My God is my rock, in whom I take refuge, my shield and the horn of my salvation. He is my stronghold, my refuge and my savior – and I am saved from my enemies" (2 Samuel 22:3).

"The Lord is a refuge for the oppressed, a stronghold in times of trouble" (Psalm 9:9).

"The Lord is my light and my salvation – whom shall I fear? The Lord is the stronghold of my life – of whom shall I be afraid?" (Psalm 27:1)

"He is my loving God and my fortress, my stronghold and my deliverer" (Psalm 144:2a).

Let God Break Out Of You

One day I woke up and I had just had a dream where I was praying over someone because I had seen him down and the enemy had piled rocks and stones and all kinds of leaves, dead grass, and junk on him and with the rain it had become stuck to him and was weighing him down and keeping him bound.

When I woke up the words "break out" came to me. I realized that this man needed to break out from all the junk that the enemy had been putting on him. The junk was the lies of the enemy which brought negative thinking and negative emotions and wrong choices. He needed to make right choices by believing the truth in God's Word and not the lies of the enemy. I realized that there was some junk that the enemy was putting on me too (some lies) that I needed to break out of as well. I needed to start picking at the junk (lies) and removing it from my life with the help of the Holy Spirit and the grace of God. Because of a difficult situation in my life at that time, I realized that I had allowed some bitterness to creep into my heart unknowingly. I also realized at that time that I was experiencing some depression and oppression in my life. I had unknowingly started to listen to the lies of the enemy and I felt bound. God's Word says that the truth sets us free. In the midst of this storm in my life I realized I needed to make a choice to receive and believe the truth and not the lies so that I could walk in the freedom that Jesus died to give me.

Can you allow the Holy Spirit to reveal the lies of the enemy that you might be believing. He reveals these lies not to condemn you because condemnation does not come from Him. It comes from the enemy. He reveals these lies to set you free from them. He is in the business of setting the captives free; that is why Jesus came. He came to set you free. You just read that in the beginning of this Book in Isaiah 61:1-3.

This person in my dream was bound by all these lies that were stuck to him. Jesus came to free us from the lies of the enemy. He came to release us from captivity, to replace these lies with truth that will turn our mourning into gladness, our ashes into beauty and our despair into praise. When we believe the truth, it will set us free. Truth will cause us to break out of the lies.

Jesus wants you free. He wants to replace the lies that you are believing with truth but you have to cooperate with Him in order for Him to do this.

I am going to say some things that may challenge your mind-sets. In order for the Holy Spirit to free you, you will have to make a choice to allow Him to bring your **mindsets** in line with His Word. I am not saying that your mindsets are wrong. I am only suggesting that you may have some wrong mindsets. Allow Him to reveal any wrong mindsets to you that you may have. Don't resist Him. For years I prayed and asked God to turn my thinking that was upside down, right side up. I pray that you will make this your prayer today. When the Holy Spirit began to change my mindsets, I almost shut Him down but then I prayed "Lord if this is truth, I want to believe it. Set me free from the lies that I have been believing." We need God to change our mindsets. Only He can do this but we have to give Him the permission to do it.

I had a mindset that needed to be changed. When I was younger and before I became a Christian, I saw God the Father as a harsh judge who was ready to pronounce judgment on me the moment I did something wrong. After I became a Christian, God began to change my mindset/my wrong perception of Him and He replaced it with truth. I don't see God the Father like that anymore. I now see Him as a loving Father who wants His very best for me. I know I can jump up on His lap at any time and receive His hugs and kisses. I can come to Him with any problem or need in my life and ask Him for advice, direction and provision. I can come boldly before His throne of grace to receive help and grace in times of need. This is how He wants us to see Him. He is very approachable. He wants a great relationship with us. The enemy wants us to think He is a harsh God who is demanding, judgmental and condemning so that we will not run to Him. John 3:17 says "For God did not send his Son into the world to condemn the world, but to save the world through him." God the Father loves us so much that He sent His one and only beloved Son into the world to die for us that we may receive forgiveness of our sins, live for Jesus and spend eternity in heaven with Him.

Saul (now known as Paul who wrote most of the New Testament) had a mindset that needed to be changed. Saul was on his way to Damascus to arrest followers of Jesus and to imprison them. Saul was brought up under the law. He was a Pharisee of Pharisees. He was very zealous for the law and because of his zeal for God he was persecuting those who believed in Jesus and who were embracing the grace of God. Jesus appeared to him and said "Saul, Saul, why do you persecute **me**?" Jesus took the persecution that Saul directed at His followers as if it was being done to Him personally.

Saul's mindset was drastically changed and he was transformed from his encounter with Jesus. After his Damascus Road experience with Jesus he became a follower of Jesus and stopped persecuting Christians. Instead he began to preach the message of grace.

God chose Paul (previously known as Saul) & Barnabas to carry His Name before the Gentiles and Jews and to bring them the good news of Jesus Christ which was the message of His grace (see Acts 13:2, 5 & 14:3). In Acts 14:3 we see that signs and wonders followed the message of God's grace that Paul was proclaiming. We see again in Acts 20:24b that Paul was given the task of testifying to the Gospel of God's grace. In Acts 20:32 Paul committed the Church to God and to the word of His grace. Paul opened and closed most of his letters with the grace and peace of God. Paul says that grace will build you up and give you an inheritance among those who are sanctified (see Acts 20:32). Instead of preaching and teaching the law, Paul was now speaking boldly the message of God's grace. So we see that God changed his mindset from being so zealous for the law and persecuting Christians to becoming a Christian himself, preaching the Gospel of Grace and being zealous for Jesus.

Peter had an encounter with God that transformed and drastically changed his mindset. Peter was also very diligent in obeying the law of Moses. One day Peter fell into a trance and he saw heaven open up and something like a large sheet come down from heaven to earth which contained all kinds of unclean animals, reptiles and birds. According to the law of Moses, the Israelites were not allowed to eat them or they would be unclean before God. In the trance (vision), God told Peter to kill and eat them and Peter said he would not because he had never eaten anything impure or unclean. God told Peter not to call anything impure that He has made clean. This happened three times (see Acts 10:9-16). God gave this vision to Peter to prepare him for what God was about to reveal to him. God was in the process of changing Peter's mindset. At that time, there was a Gentile man by the name of Cornelius that sent for Peter to come to him so that he and his family could hear what God commanded Peter to tell them. Just as the men that Cornelius had sent to get Peter arrived, the Holy Spirit told Peter that they had come and that he was to go with them. Peter went to Cornelius' house and told them that it was against the law for a Jew to associate with a Gentile or visit him but God had shown him not to call any man impure or unclean. He then understood the vision God had given to him and realized that, because of Jesus' redemptive work, God will accept everyone who believes (see Acts 10:34-35). Up until that time Peter had thought that salvation was only for the Jews. Peter then told Cornelius and his family the good news about Jesus and because they believed they were all baptized in the Holy Spirit with evidence of speaking in tongues (see Acts 10:17-46). God, who knows the heart, showed that He accepted them by giving the Holy Spirit to them just as He did to the Jews (see Acts 15:8). Peter told them about the good news of Jesus Christ which is the Gospel of Grace. Peter never said anything to them about obeying the law of Moses. He only told them to believe in Jesus and receive forgiveness of their sins through His name (see Acts 10:43).

Remember I said in the dream I had, that the person I was praying over was down and the enemy had piled rocks and stones and all kinds of leaves, dead grass and junk on him and with the rain it had become stuck to him and was weighing him down and keeping him bound. I said that the junk was the lies of the enemy that he had believed. A lie that the enemy tries to get us to believe is that we, as believers in Jesus Christ, are still under the law of Moses.

I was one of those believers that the enemy lied to. I had a wrong mindset that God wanted to change and bring in line with His Word so that I could experience freedom in my life. Jesus paid such a huge price to set me free and I was not walking completely in that freedom that He died to give me. I was walking in a mixture of grace and the law but God wanted me to walk in grace alone. Because I was walking under the law at times, I was also walking in self-righteousness as they go hand in hand but God wanted me to only walk in His righteousness. When we walk under the law, we are walking in self-righteousness because we still think we can earn God's blessings through what we do. I hadn't realized that sometimes I was still walking under the law and self-righteousness until God showed me. I hadn't realized that my wrong mindsets were holding me in bondage to negative emotions.

God promises that if I receive His abundant provision of grace and His gift of righteousness, I will reign in life through Jesus Christ (see Romans 5:17b). Making the choice to receive God's pure unadulterated grace and His gift of righteousness is the turning around point to breaking out from that bondage of lies and from wrong mindsets. This is a choice we need to make every day of our lives. It will destroy those chains of bondage. It will destroy those religious mindsets. It will remove the weight, the heaviness and cause us to break out in praise to God. God has used the message of grace in my life and the truth that I am the righteousness of God in Christ Jesus to set me free from many things including sorrow.

God sets us free and then the enemy tries to take us down into that pit again. He tries to do this you know. When those thoughts of despair would come to me and I would actually feel myself descending downward towards that pit, I would pray Romans 5:17b. "Father, in Jesus' Name, I receive Your abundant provision of grace and Your gift of righteousness to reign in life through Jesus Christ." This is my life line when the enemy attacks. I also pray and ask the Holy Spirit to keep me from going down into that pit and He does. There have been a few times when I did go down into the pit but as

I continued to focus on Jesus and continued to receive His grace and His righteousness and remembered the things I am teaching you in this Book, I would find myself standing on the solid Rock of Jesus Christ once again.

To know that I am righteous means that even when I feel wrong, I am still right with God simply because I believe in Jesus, His Son. I have meditated on the truth that I am the righteousness of God in Christ Jesus many times to get my wrong mindset and my wrong thinking turned right side up. He gave me His righteousness. I can't get any more righteous. I need to believe this truth by faith. This will put an end to condemnation. Romans 8:1 says "Therefore, there is no condemnation for those who are in Christ Jesus". We need to believe this even when we don't do everything right. When we believe by faith that we are the righteousness of God in Christ Jesus, the enemy doesn't have any weapon to use against us. He has lost his power.

When you are in a situation and you need God's help, **receive** His grace and then make the choice to speak out His Word over your life and your situation. When you do this you are a candidate for God to pour out His grace and His power in your life. No matter how hard it is, start to thank God for His love. Say "Thank you Father God that you love me. Thank you Jesus that you love me and that you care about me. Thank you Holy Spirit for Your grace and power in my life to turn my thinking/believing around." Ask Him to help you stop thinking about and talking about all your problems and to start speaking out the Word of God that you need to hear. Then make the choice and open your mouth and start speaking out God's promises. God doesn't hold back these promises. We do by our wrong thinking/ believing which results in wrong choices. As our thinking/believing is turned around, so will our choices be turned around.

Throughout this Book you will find many promises from God's Word for you to declare. Whatever you need and want that is in accordance with His Will for you, **ask God for it**. His Will is for you to be free and for you to enjoy your life. We read that in Isaiah 61. The whole purpose of Jesus coming to earth, suffering for us and dying for us was to set us free.

If you have made wrong choices, do not condemn yourself. Forgive yourself and move on with Jesus. We have all made wrong choices in life.

Ask God to give you a desire for His Word so that you can know Him more and more. That's my heart. Sometimes I have to pray and ask God to draw me to His Word because I don't feel like getting into His Word. Instead of condemning myself, I pray and put the matter in God's hands and when I feel His prompting, I need to make the choice to say "Yes, Lord".

Getting to know our God through His Word does not make us more acceptable to God but it does give us **ammunition** against the enemy.

By reading God's Word, we can look at it as spending time with the One who loves us and wanting to get to know Him better and better. Paul prayed in Ephesians 1:17-19 that we would have the spirit of wisdom and revelation so that we would know Him better and that the eyes of our hearts would be enlightened in order that we may know the hope to which He called us, the riches of His glorious inheritance in the saints and His incomparably great power for us who believe.

He also prayed in Ephesians 3:16-19 that out of His glorious riches of grace that we would be strengthened with His power by His Spirit so that Christ would dwell in our hearts through faith and then he goes on to pray that we would grasp how wide and long and high and deep is the love of Christ for us (personally) and that we would know His love for us (by experience) so that we would be **filled** to the measure of all the fullness of God, that we would be filled with all His fullness, that we would be full of God Himself.

Then he states that God is able to do immeasurably, exceedingly, abundantly, above and beyond all that we would ever ask, imagine or think according to His great power that is at work within us (see Ephesians 3:20). Did you see that? It is God's great power that lives in us that will do it. The more we know the Word of God, the more we will have God's Word in our hearts and the more His Word will come out of our mouth. It will **break out of our mouth.** The more we are strengthened by His Spirit, the more power we will have. The more we receive the love of God for us personally and know it by experience, the fuller we will be filled with God Himself and the more supernatural and miraculous things that only God can do (things we cannot imagine or think of ourselves) will break out in our lives because of His great power that is at work within us. It will come from within us. **Break out is letting God's Word break out of us.** It is letting His Truth break out of us. Jesus is Truth and He is in us. Allow Truth to get so big in us that He breaks out of us.

God has already done everything He can do to break us out of the lies of the enemy (emotional bondage). Jesus accomplished the victory for us on the cross. When He said "It is finished" He was saying that He made everything available to those who would believe and receive. God is no respecter of persons. What He already did for one, He did for all. All we need to do is to believe that He did it all for us and to receive what He did. Of course, we need to find out what He did for us so that we can believe it and receive it. We need to trust Him to guide us by His Spirit and then do what His Spirit is telling us to do one day at a time. It is that simple. We may make some mistakes along the way thinking it is the Holy Spirit when it might be our own wants and desires that we are following but don't get discouraged because we are all learning how to be led by God's Spirit. We have all made mistakes. I know I have.

There is a battle that is going on in our minds and the way out is to **fight the good fight of faith**. That is our battle. Our battle is not the enemy. Jesus has already defeated our enemy for us. We don't have to defeat him, although there are times we need to use our authority over him to enforce what Jesus has already done. Our battle is not to get rid of the sin in our lives because Jesus has already forgiven us for all our sins, past, present and future sins. God does not want us sin conscious. The devil wants us sin conscious. God wants us righteousness conscious because that is where the victory is. He wants our focus on Him not on our shortcomings. When we focus on our sins, this will defeat us! We are not set free from sin by being sin conscious (focusing on our sins) any more than we are set free from lack by being poverty conscious or from disease by being disease conscious. We are set free from all these things by being Jesus conscious. Focus on Jesus, your Righteous. Focus on the truth that you are as righteous as Jesus is because He gave you His righteousness.

This will cause us to break out! Our battle is to **believe** in Jesus and in His finished work on the cross. Our battle is to **believe** that satan is defeated by the blood of the Lamb. Plead the blood of Jesus over your emotions. Our battle is to **believe** that all our sins have been forgiven and the punishment for those sins taken for us by Jesus Himself on the cross. **Our battle is to fight the good fight of faith** and we fight this fight with the faith of the Son of God. The problem is we have been trying to fight it with our own faith. His faith resides in us because Jesus resides in us.

This next statement is a truth that set me free from struggling to have faith in God. So listen closely. This fight of faith is to simply continue to believe in Jesus and in what He has already done for you. Find out what He has done for you in His Word and simply choose to believe it. This will bring about a divine rest in Him. In Hebrews Chapter 3 God said that they would never enter His rest because of unbelief. To rest is to believe in Jesus. It isn't about your faithfulness. It is about His faithfulness. He is faithful. Believe that He is faithful.

You may be trying with all your efforts to do all the right things to be acceptable to God. God accepts you just the way you are because you believe in Jesus. God wants you to believe right which will lead to right living automatically. You may have been trying so hard to set yourself free from sin, sorrow, etc. You cannot set yourself free. The problem is not with wrong living. The **root of the problem is your wrong believing, your wrong mindsets**. When you believe right, you will do right. If you believe wrong, you will do wrong. God is not interested in behavior modification that doesn't last. He came to bring transformation and this will automatically take place when you renew your mind with His Word and believe right. It takes time to get our minds renewed with God's Word. In fact, our minds will continue to be renewed with His Word for the remainder of our lives. So don't beat yourself up because you are not doing everything right. Allow God's Word to bring the transformation. This Book is designed to reveal spiritual truths to you from God's Word in each chapter that will help you to believe right and to see what belongs to you, as a child of God.

When you read the Word, **believe and receive** what the Word of God says about who you are in Christ. Apply it to your life. Meditate on it. This will bring break out.

21

The Word says "God is love". His love is our inheritance in Christ Jesus. Did you know that? I really believe God is emphasizing to the Church in these last days His love for us. He wants us to receive His love and believe He loves us personally and perfectly. He wants to anchor us in His love. He wants us rooted and grounded in His love. I have dedicated a whole Chapter in this Book on God's love for us. Because of the times we are in, it is so important that we are anchored in His love. When our faith is tested, because we know the love of God for us personally and by experience, we will stand firm in Christ.

I have listed some choices that you need to make to experience break out from wrong mindsets and the lies and deception of the enemy. I pray you will make these choices in your heart as you read them. I recommend that you read them out loud so that you can hear yourself. When you hear yourself making these choices, it will have a positive effect on your heart. These choices will be your turning around point. By making these choices, it doesn't mean that you will always make the right choices in your life. If you make some wrong choices, don't let the enemy condemn you and lead you away from Jesus. Even when you make wrong choices, you can choose to turn from those wrong choices and make right choices by faith. **By faith we make these choices**. Jesus knows what you need. Let Him set you free.

The following are some choices you can make:

By faith, I choose to give Jesus all my bitterness, negative emotions, hurts, wounds, pride, lack, selfishness, self-pity and wrong mindsets and I choose to lay these things at the foot of the cross and to receive His healing, deliverance, freedom, wholeness, provision and right mindsets. I choose to allow God to heal my broken wounded heart. I choose to believe that God is for me and not against me. I choose to receive God's grace (His unmerited favor, unearned favor, undeserved favor) for me. I choose to read the Word of God through the lens of grace and not the lens of the law. I choose to receive God's acceptance of me even when man rejects me. I choose to receive God's righteousness even when I have just done something awful. I choose to believe that I am the righteousness of God in Christ Jesus by faith. By believing this I am removing the enemy's weapon of condemnation. I choose to receive forgiveness of all my sins (past, present and future sins). I choose to receive God's forgiveness even when I have just sinned. I choose to walk out the salvation of my soul the same way I got saved, by grace through faith in Jesus Christ. I choose to receive God's perfect love for me. I choose to believe that God cares about me and wants His best for me. I choose to enjoy my life in the Holy Spirit. I choose to renew my mind with the Word of God. I choose to stop listening to the lies of the enemy and to start believing what God says about me and my situation. I choose to see myself through God's eyes of love. I choose to stop allowing the enemy to oppress me and to keep me thinking about and talking about all the negative things that have happened to me. I choose to receive God's free gift of no condemnation. I choose to believe that Jesus set me free from condemnation to go and sin no more. I choose to believe right so that right living will follow. I choose to trust the Holy Spirit to guide me into God's Word and to teach me who I am in Christ and to help me grasp the love and grace of God for me personally and to know His Will for my life. I choose to be led by the Holy Spirit. I choose to allow my new nature to dominate me. I choose to make Jesus my Bridegroom. I choose to keep my focus on Jesus and to do things His way one day at a time. By faith, no matter what happens in my life, I make the choice to always believe in Jesus. By faith, I choose to lay down my will, my wants and my desires and I choose to receive and embrace God's Will and desires for my life. I choose to believe that God's Will and desires for my life are much better than mine.

These are only a few of the choices we can make. We are faced with many choices every day of our lives. Making the right choices should not be burdensome when we receive God's grace to do it. Jesus said that His yoke is easy and His burden is light.

Now please take a few minutes to declare who you are in Christ Jesus. When you make declarations, you are saying "This is what I believe". Don't just rattle on mindlessly. Put your heart into it. Think about what you are declaring. This is what I believe!!!!!

We need to start speaking out what God thinks about us regularly. We need to start seeing ourselves the way God sees us. God wants us to receive freely from Him without thinking we have to

23

earn His blessings or that we have to be perfect before we can receive His blessings. Grace is undeserved, unearned, unmerited favor of God. We cannot deserve, earn or merit His favor. It must be received by faith.

As you make the following declarations, allow Jesus to get so big in you that He breaks out of you.

I am the righteousness of God in Christ Jesus even when I feel angry or have just sinned. Thank You Jesus that you have made me righteous. I am accepted by You, Jesus, simply because I believe in You. Thank You Jesus that you accept me just the way I am. I am a new creation in Christ Jesus. I have been made new. The old is gone and the new has come. Thank You Jesus, I have Your divine nature in me and Your nature is love. I am Your precious child. I belong to You Lord Jesus. I am cherished in Your sight. I am valuable to You. I am the apple of Your eye. I am treasured by You. I am chosen by You. I am important to You. You love me with an undying uncondi-tional love! You will never stop loving me. I am filled with the full measure of God Himself. I am a carrier of Your Presence. Jesus, You are my good Shepherd. You are good to me all the time. I receive Your goodness. I follow You and only You. You have forgiven me of all my sins (past, present and future sins). Jesus, You have already given me the victory over sin. I believe this by faith. You have set me upon the Rock. Jesus, You are my Rock. I am secure in You. You are the anchor for my soul. You are my stronghold, my fortress, my refuge, my rescuer, my deliverer, my healer, my abundant provider, my Savior, my Lord and my life. You are my all in all, my everything. You mean everything to me. I am amply supplied. I have more than enough. You take what I have and You multiply it with leftovers. I have the victory already because Jesus You are my Victor. I trust You Jesus with my life. You protect me and my family. You are my resting place. I can rest in You because I trust You. I don't have to fix the problem in my life. I receive Your grace and I trust You to do it. I am getting out of the way and letting You be God in my life. I have been enriched in every way because I receive Your grace. I do not lack any blessing. You keep me strong to the end because You are faithful. I have the mind of Christ, a sound mind, a whole mind, a peaceful mind, a loving mind, a blessed mind, a joyful mind, a Spirit led mind. I am seated with You, Jesus, as a co-heir, at the right hand of God the Father far above all rule and authority, power and dominion of the enemy. All negative emotions are under my feet. Because I receive Your grace, miracles and the supernatural are taking place in my life. Thank you Jesus I receive everything from You that I need for life and godliness.

Now stand up and shout to God with a voice of triumphant!!!

The Salvation
Of Your Soul Brings Joy

*"**With joy** you will draw water from the wells of salvation" (Isaiah 12:3 emphasis added).*

We know that God is our only Savior. We know that there is only one God and He consists of three persons: Father, Son, and Holy Spirit. We are made in His image (see Genesis 2:26 -27) and, therefore, we are also a three part being: spirit, soul and body. God wants to bring salvation to all three parts of us. Ephesians 2:8 says that it is by grace we are saved through faith – and this not from ourselves, it is the gift of God – not by works, so that no one can boast. When we accept Jesus into our lives, our spirit is completely saved and made right with God. Our spirit is perfect before Him. The salvation of our spirit is by grace through faith. However, our soul and body are in the process of being saved. Our soul is our mind (our thoughts), our will and **our emotions** which flow out of our heart. God wants to save our soul and our body as well. **Just like our Spirit is saved by grace through faith, our soul is saved the same way.** Our soul is saved by grace through faith, not by grace through our works. **The salvation of our soul is the renewing of our minds with God's Word** which results in us knowing who we are in Christ and receiving His finished works by faith. Our minds are renewed as we believe God's Word. Jesus has already done everything for us in

His redemptive work. What we need to do is believe it and receive it. This will result in healed **emotions**, healed body, healed mind and wholeness in every area of our life. Now this is good news!

If I think I can save my own soul by good works and while trying having some success, I will boast in myself but when God does it, I will boast about Him. The salvation of my soul does not come from my works but rather it is when my mind is renewed with God's Word and my actions follow my right believing.

Prayer: Father, in Jesus' Name, thank You for saving my spirit, soul and body and for bringing me into the fullness of what you have for me. I now realize that just as my spirit was saved by grace through faith, my soul is also saved the same way, by grace through faith. Please help me to renew my mind (which is the salvation of my soul) with Your Word so that I may enjoy You and experience healed emotions, etc. in my life.

As you read the next scripture, pay attention to what God does for us.

> *"The **Lord** is my shepherd. I shall not be in want. **He** makes me lie down in green pastures, **he** leads me beside quiet waters, **he restores my soul**. **He** guides me in paths of righteousness for his name's sake. Even though I walk through the valley of the shadow of death, I will fear no evil, for **you** are with me; **your** rod and **your** staff they comfort me. **You** prepare a table before me in the presence of my enemies. **You** anoint my head with oil, my cup overflows" (Psalm 23:1-5, emphasis added).*

Did you notice that God is doing all these things? This is all being done by God to restore our soul. He says He will restore my soul. He says He will restore your soul. Our part is to simply believe in Him.

> *"As the deer pants for streams of water, so **my soul** pants for you, O God. **My soul** thirsts for God, for the living God. When can I go and meet with God?" (Psalm 42:1-2, emphasis added)*

As we receive this great salvation of our soul by grace through faith in Jesus, we will realize just how great our God is and our soul will long for more and more of Him. Our soul will be turned more and more to God. As we receive His grace and His righteousness firsthand, our soul will respond to God. As we experience God's manifested Presence in our lives, we will realize that His Presence is so good that we will want to be in His Presence more and more.

> *"Why are you downcast, **O my soul?** Why so disturbed within me? **Put your hope in God**, for I will yet praise him, my Savior and my God" (Psalm 42:11, emphasis added).*

If we believe the lies of the enemy, our soul will be downcast and disturbed within us. It is when we believe the lies of the enemy that our souls are burdened. For example: You're no good. You will never amount to anything. You aren't saved. Look at how you acted. God doesn't love you. God doesn't accept you. You will never be healed. You will never be made whole. You will never be free from sorrow, addiction, etc. These are the lies of the enemy to keep our soul in bondage to him. The Psalmist says to put your hope in God for He is your Savior and your God. Look to Jesus and keep looking to Jesus alone for your victory.

Prayer: Father, in Jesus' Name, I put my hope in You alone for You are my Savior and my God.

> *"Find rest, O my soul, in **God alone**; my hope comes from him. **He alone** is my rock and my salvation; **he** is my fortress, I will not be shaken. My salvation and my honor depend on **God**; **he** is my mighty rock, my refuge. Trust in **him** at all times, O people; pour out your hearts to **him**, for **God** is our refuge" (Psalm 62:5-8, emphasis added).*

What is your soul saying to you? Your soul should not be thinking of or speaking out negative things about yourself but rather it should be saying: God alone is my rest, my hope, my rock, my salvation, my fortress, my protection, my stability, my refuge, my deliverer, my peace and my joy. If your soul is speaking out the negative, keep reading this Book so that your thinking and your believing will come in line with God's Word. God wants us to speak life over ourselves.

Trust in God. Don't trust in yourself or in your works. Knowing and believing that God is all these things to you personally is part of the salvation of your soul. These things are part of your inheritance in Christ Jesus. They belong to you as a child of God. In order for you to benefit from them, you must believe that they belong to you and receive them. Your part is to believe, with childlike faith, in Jesus as your personal Savior and Lord and receive His benefits. He doesn't hold them back. He freely gives us all things. He is a good Father.

God wants to see us in a stable place. He wants to see us walking on level ground. He doesn't want us to be up one day and down the next day. Jesus came to set us free from the roller coaster ride and to stabilize us. He is our Rock upon whom we stand.

> *"I will praise you as long as I live, and in your name I will lift up my hands. **My soul will be satisfied** with the richest of foods; with singing lips my mouth will praise you. On my bed, **I remember you: I think of you** through the watches of the night. **Because you are my help**, I sing in the shadow of your wings. **My soul clings to you; your right hand upholds me"** (Psalm 63:4-8, emphasis added).*

Is your soul satisfied? This scripture says that my soul will be satisfied as I meditate (remember, think) on Jesus and all He has done for me and as I sing His praises. It says that my soul clings to God and He upholds me and I am wonderfully saved. Praising God, singing to God and mediating on God is for our benefit. Does God enjoy our praise? Absolutely yes! God enjoys it when we praise Him. It touches His heart and His heart skips a beat. He enjoys our fellowship tremendously but we are the ones who will benefit the most from praising God. Our soul needs to praise Him. Something happens within our soul when we praise God.

If you are having difficulty praising God, talk to Him about it. Don't condemn yourself. Ask God to help you to praise Him. You can start by reading Psalms 145 to 150 as these psalms will help you to praise God. You can turn them into praise.

> *"When anxiety was great within me, your consolation brought joy to my soul" (Psalm 94:19).*

God comforts me and sets me free from all negative emotions and this brings joy to my soul. Comfort is another part of my inheritance in Christ Jesus. He comforts me with a comfort that only He can give. No one else can comfort me like Jesus can. Child of God receive His comfort today and as often as you need it.

> *"Praise the Lord, **O my soul**; all my inmost being, praise his holy name. Praise the Lord, **O my soul**, and forget not all his benefits – who forgives all your sins and heals all your diseases, who redeems your life from the pit and crowns you with love and compassion, who satisfies your desires with good things so that your youth is renewed like the eagles" (Psalm 103:1-6, emphasis added).*

We can speak to our soul just like David did in Psalm 103. We can tell our soul to praise God and to remember all His benefits. When we remember His benefits, we are, in fact, praising God. Have you ever thought about this before? These benefits are part of our inheritance in Christ Jesus. What are they again:

1. All my sins are forgiven;
2. All my diseases are healed;
3. My life is redeemed from the pit;
4. I am crowned with love and compassion;
5. I am satisfied with good things; and
6. My youth is renewed like the eagles.

This is something to praise God about. No wonder the Psalmist said "Praise the Lord, O my soul; all my inmost being, praise his holy name".

> *"Pleasant words are a honeycomb, sweet to the*
> *soul and healing to the bones" (Proverbs 16:24,*
> *emphasis added).*

Think about words that have been spoken over you that are pleasant for they will bring to you healing, encouragement, life, joy, energy, singing, impartation and wholeness. Allow God to circumcise your heart from all words of death, rejection, guilt, condemnation and shame. Ask Him to cut these things out of your soul. God says in Deuteronomy 30:6 that He will circumcise your heart so that you can love Him with all your soul. **He will** cut away, destroy and remove everything in your soul (your mind, will and emotions) that is meant to destroy you for these things will keep you from fulfilling God's plans and purposes in your life. You simply have to turn towards Him and ask Him to do it and then be patient and allow Him freedom in your life. His plans for you are always for your good.

Please agree with me as I pray the following prayer over you.

Father I come in agreement with my brother or sister and ask that You would circumcise their heart from all negative words spoken over them that have resulted in negative emotions, and heal their wounded heart. Replace these negative words with the truth in Your Word. Help them to see themselves and love themselves the way Jesus sees and loves them, in Jesus' Name.

> *"For I know the plans I have for you, declares the Lord,*
> *plans to prosper you and not to harm you, plans to*
> *give you hope and a future" (Jeremiah 29:11).*

When we know that God is for us and not against us and that He has great plans for us, it brings joy to our soul.

> *"Come to me, all you who are weary and burdened,*
> *and I will give you rest. Take my yoke upon you and*

*learn from me, for I am gentle and humble in heart,
and you will **find rest for your souls**. **For my yoke
is easy and my burden is light**" (Matthew 11:28-30,
emphasis added).*

Jesus wants us to rest in Him and wait upon Him. He wants us to
give our heavy burdens to Him and receive His yoke which is easy
and His burden which is light.

Years ago my husband and I purchased a business. Although we
prayed about it, we ran ahead of God and purchased the wrong business. We did not wait for God to show us what business to purchase.
I did not have peace but we purchased it anyway. It was 6 ½ years
of struggles to say the least. We did not know what we know now
and so we were constantly trying to make things happen in our own
power and strength. We would try this and we would try that and all
we were doing was making ourselves busy with very little, if anything, to show from all our hard work.

Are you weary and burdened? Are you tired? Ask God to reveal
to you what it is that you are doing in order to try to please Him or
doing out of a sense of duty that He has not asked you to do or, perhaps, isn't His timing. In the Old Testament, God led the Israelites
by a pillar of fire through the night and by a cloud through the day.
The Israelites only moved when the cloud or the pillar of fire moved.
Otherwise, they stayed put. Lay all your self-efforts, your plans and
your timetable at the foot of the Cross and while you are waiting for
God's direction abide (dwell) at the Cross to find rest for your soul.
Be still and know that He is God. Cease striving in your own power.
Get to know Him intimately. Wait on Him until He invites you to
join Him in what He is already doing. God never asked you to decide
what you would do for Him. God is not obligated to bless what He
has not first initiated or instructed you to do. When you join Him at
His invitation, it is His timing, and whatever He invites you to do will
bear much fruit for His Kingdom and it will bring joy to your soul.

God wants us to be willing to lay down our self-efforts, our plans
and our agendas and wait upon Him to receive His plans and His
agenda for our lives. This is part of the salvation of our soul. It is the
salvation of our will.

> *"I will give you a new heart and put a new spirit in you; I will remove from you your **heart of stone** and give you a **heart of flesh**. And I will put **my Spirit** in you and **move you** to follow my decrees and be careful to keep my laws" (Ezekiel 36:26-27, emphasis added).*

Ezekiel was speaking prophetically into the future when we would believe in Jesus. This is what takes place spiritually when we first believe in Jesus. God said He would remove our heart of stone and give us a heart of flesh. He said that He would do it. Spiritually speaking, because we believe in Jesus and in His finished work, God has given us a heart transplant. He has removed our heart of stone (unbelief) and replaced it with His Son's heart. We now have Jesus' heart beating in us. Just like a heart transplant recipient has a new heart and it is the heart of another person beating in them, we have Jesus' heart beating in us. Think about this.

From the scriptures we looked at in this Chapter, what is the salvation of our soul?

It is knowing that God comforts me, heals my mind and emotions, pours His love into my soul, restores me, rescues me from the enemies schemes, refreshes me, lifts me up out of the pit (depression, discouragement, sorrow, etc.), crowns me with love and compassion, and upholds me. It is when my soul boasts in the Lord and offers Him my praise because of who He is to me personally. It is when I gaze upon Jesus and His beauty fills my soul. It is when my soul finds rest in God alone by taking upon myself Jesus' yoke which is easy and His burden which is light. It is when I stop struggling in my own power and strength. It is when my soul thirsts for God and is satisfied by His Word, is strengthened and finds contentment in God alone. It is when my soul rests in the satisfaction that only Jesus can give. It is when I let Him take the reins in my life and wait upon Him to lead me instead of running ahead of Him or lagging behind Him. It is knowing that God is my hope, my rock upon which I will stand, my eternal salvation, my fortress, my shield, my stability and my refuge and that I can run to Him no matter what I have done. It is knowing that all my sins are forgiven, all my diseases are healed (this includes my emotions) and all my desires are satisfied in Him.

It is when I know that God accepts me and loves me just the way I am. It is seeing myself the way God sees me through His eyes of love and being able to see others through those same eyes of love. It is knowing that God is my hope and that He has a good future for me. It is when I allow God to circumcise my heart and He cuts away, destroys and removes those things that are meant to destroy me. It is when I find freedom and wholeness in my blessed Savior. It is knowing that God has removed my heart of stone and replaced it with Jesus' heart. It is knowing that Jesus' heart is beating in me. To sum it up, it is when my mind is renewed with God's Word which results in right believing and right actions.

Everyone is at a unique place in the salvation of our soul. It is a journey that we are all on until we meet the Lord face to face. God wants us to enjoy the journey!

Knowing And Experiencing
God's Love Brings Joy

I have come to realize that it is so important that I **know personally** just how much God loves me and equally important to **receive** His love for me. It isn't good enough just to know that the scriptures say that God loves me. I need to believe that He loves me. I need to receive His love and experience His love for me first hand and so do you. It is so vitally important that we are anchored in His love.

Ask yourself this question. Is my sorrow, fear based? I asked myself this question and to be honest there were times that the sorrow I was experiencing was fear based.

The Bible says that perfect love casts out all fear. Let's look at that scripture.

> *"And so we rely on the love God has for us.* ***God is*** *
> ***love****. Whoever lives in love lives in God, and God in*
> *him. Love is made complete among us so that we will*
> *have confidence on the day of judgment, because in*
> *this world we are like him. There is no fear in love.*
> ***But perfect love drives out fear****, because fear has to*
> *do with punishment. The man who fears is not made*
> *perfect in love" (1 John 4:16-18, emphasis added).*

In my early Christian years I used to think that if I had fears, my love was not made perfect. That was a wrong belief. This scripture is not referring to my love being perfect. Rather, it refers to God's love that is perfect. So if you have fears in your heart, you need to know God's perfect love for you. You need to believe and receive God's love for you. When you know God's perfect love for you, it will drive fear far from you.

To the degree that you have received God's love for you, will be the degree of freedom you have from fear because perfect love drives out fear. God is love. Did you see that in this scripture? God **is** love. There is no love apart from God. He is the source of love. He is the embodiment of love. There would not be any love if it weren't for God. If you have any love in your heart, it is because God first loved you and deposited His love into your heart. You need to get a revelation of God's love for you personally. Receive God's love for you and keep receiving it throughout your life and the enemy will not be able to rob you of joy.

I want you to see something else from this scripture. It says that "love is made complete among us so that we will have confidence on the day of judgment". What is this day of judgment and why can we have confidence on that day? The Bible talks about a day when God will judge the world for their sins. However, this day of judgment is not for the believer. It is only for the unbeliever. As a believer, all our sins are forgiven the moment we accept Jesus into our life as our personal Savior and Lord. Jesus took upon Himself on the cross all our sins, as if He committed them Himself, and all our punishment for our sins (see Isaiah 53:4-5). Our sins are forgiven and we will no longer be punished by God for our sins because of Jesus' redemptive work for us. This is our confidence on the day of judgment.

Now this scripture also says "fear has to do with punishment". As a believer, we can experience fear because we do not understand God's perfect love towards us and we may think that God is like a judge who is ready to pronounce judgement (or punishment) upon us the moment we do something wrong. As long as we, as believers, think God is going to punish us for our sins, then we will walk in fear because we have not yet experienced God's perfect love for us. As long as we **believe in Jesus**, we will never be punished for our sins. In fact, the only sin that God punishes, is the sin of rejecting His Son. Jesus has already taken upon Himself all of God's wrath for our sins. Jesus went to hell in our place so as to satisfy the full wrath of God for us. My friends, get a hold of this truth. The truth is you are forgiven for all your sins because you believe in Jesus.

The only judgment that a believer will come before God for is the judgment of our works. If our works are like gold, silver and precious stones we will be rewarded by God. However, if our works are like wood, hay and stubble we will suffer loss of rewards. Our works determine our rewards in heaven (see 1 Corinthians 3:10-15). If we work to be acceptable to God, to be loved by God, to be noticed by man or do works with a wrong heart motive, these are works that are like wood, hay and stubble and these will be burned up on the day of judgment. We will receive no reward for these works. However, if the works we do flow out of our believing in Jesus and we do them because we are motivated by His love for us and want to see His Kingdom increase, these are works that are like gold, silver and precious stones. We will receive a reward for these works on the day of judgment.

Now let's look at the Apostle John's revelation of God's love for Him personally. John believed and declared that He was loved. We know scripture says that John was the disciple who Jesus loved. Right! We are familiar with this scripture. Do you know where this scripture is found? Let me tell you. It is found in the Gospel written by John. John, himself, declared it in John 13:23. He says "one of them, **the disciple whom Jesus loved**, was reclining next to him."

John believed that Jesus loved him and because he believed it, he declared it. I used to think "WOW, John is the disciple who Jesus loved. He must have had a special place in Jesus' heart." This is what I thought. John had a revelation of Jesus' love for him personally. He believed that Jesus loved him and he received Jesus' love. Now that I understand and believe that Jesus loves me the same as He loved John, I can declare that "Jeannette is the disciple that Jesus loved". You can put your own name in there. You can do that now. Say your name and then say "is the disciple that Jesus loved".

I also want to point out something else in the scripture in John 13:23 where John states that he is the disciple whom Jesus loved. He goes on to say that He was reclining next to Jesus. This was at the last supper. I don't see anywhere in the scriptures where Jesus told the apostles to sit in certain seats at the Last Supper. I don't see that Jesus had reserved a seat right next to Him for John. I believe it was John who chose to sit right next to Jesus. It was John who chose to lean his head against Jesus' breast (see John 13:25). Because John believed that Jesus loved him, he wanted to be as close to Jesus as he could possibly be. My friends when we know the truth that **Jesus loves us personally**, it will lead us to stay right at His side, close to Him like John.

Peter was afraid to ask Jesus who He was talking about when He said there was one among them that would betray Him. At the Last Supper, Peter told John to ask Jesus who this betrayer was (see John 13:24). Peter was not as confident as John was that Jesus loved him. When we are confident in Jesus' love for us, we will not hesitate to ask Him anything. Nothing is too minor or too big to ask Him but in your asking always ask in accordance with God's Will for your life. His Will is always good.

Do you remember in the Bible in John 19:26 just before Jesus died, He saw His mother, Mary, and His apostle, John, standing nearby. Jesus said to John from the cross "Here is your mother". Why did Jesus pick John to say this to? I asked the Holy Spirit this question and immediately the answer came. It was because John was rooted and established in His Savior's love for him and he actually had Jesus' heart beating in him. Jesus was able to entrust John to take care of His mother. He knew that His very own love was in John. John had been receiving His love and He knew John was made full with His love and would lovingly take care of His mother.

John was the only apostle found at the foot of the cross. The Bible makes no mention of any of the other apostles even being anywhere near Jesus.

Remember the scriptures tell us that Peter denied Jesus three times after Jesus was arrested. Peter was afraid that if he admitted being Jesus' disciple that they might arrest him too. At that time in Peter's life, he did not know Jesus' love for him like John did.

When we are rooted and grounded in our Savior's love for us personally, we will not be afraid to tell the world that we are His disciple.

*"The Lord your God is with you, he is mighty to save.
He will take great delight in you, he will rejoice over
you with singing" (Zephaniah 3:17).*

God delights in you. Believe this. Receive it. Drink in His love for you personally. Don't let condemnation, guilt and shame disqualify you from receiving His love. None of us are perfect. None of us do everything perfectly all the time. We don't always make the right choices. God wants us to make right choices because wrong choices will bring negative consequences and destruction. The negative consequences and destruction do not come from God but from our wrong choices. However, when you make wrong choices don't allow the enemy to put condemnation, guilt or shame on you. Receive His love and forgiveness as this will help you make right choices going forward. God gives us the gift of no condemnation so that we can go and sin no more. You may think that your sin is too big and too unforgiveable. That is a lie from hell. Don't believe it. Jesus has already forgiven you but it is up to you to receive His forgiveness and His love. Run to Him and not away from Him. As you get to know Him better and better through His Word, as you get to know that He is for you and not against you, as you get to know who you are in Christ, as you become Jesus' conscious and not sin conscious, that sin will lose its power over you and one day you will realize you are free from it. Jesus came to set you free from the entanglement of sin. Keep your eyes focused on Him, not on your sin.

*"Satisfy us in the morning with your unfailing love,
that we may sing for joy and be glad all our days"
(Psalm 90:14).*

In order to experience the kind of joy that God wants to bless us with, we need to be satisfied with God's love. We need to grasp that God's love will never fail us.

Prayer: Father, in Jesus' Name, thank You that Your love is greater than any sorrow, sin, etc. in me. Your love, O God, is greater than any fear in me. Hallelujah! Please give me a revelation of Your love and Jesus' love for me personally and by experience and help me to recognize and receive Your love in my life on a daily basis.

> *"Who shall separate us from the love of Christ? Shall trouble or hardship or persecution or famine or nakedness or danger or sword? As it is written: "For your sake we face death all day long; we are considered as sheep to be slaughtered." No, in all these things we are more than conquerors through him who loved us. For I am convinced that neither death nor life, neither angels nor demons, neither the present nor the future, nor any powers, neither height nor depth, nor anything else in all creation, will be able to separate us from the love of God that is in Christ Jesus our Lord" (Romans 8:35-38).*

Once you know and understand God's love for you personally and have settled it in your heart that God loves you, nothing will be able to separate you from God's love. When the sorrows of life come, the enemy will not be able to lie to you and say that God does not love you. You will not believe the lie because you know and understand and have grasped the love of God for you personally. You will be able to stand firm on the Rock with Jesus as your Chief Cornerstone anchoring you with His love. His love is the anchor that will keep you firm and solid during emotional times.

> *"For **he chose us** in him before the creation of the world to be holy and blameless in his sight. In love, he predestined us to be adopted as his sons through Jesus Christ, in accordance with his pleasure and will" (Ephesians 1:4-5, emphasis added).*

God chose you before you were even conceived. God chose to adopt you into His family. Sometimes people have children that weren't planned. However, when someone adopts a child, they plan to bring this child into their family. Most of the time it is a great expense but they want a child so much that they are willing to pay the cost whatever it is. They willingly make great sacrifices in order to adopt a child. God the Father made plans to adopt you into His family and because of His great love for you He had a plan already set in motion for you to be His child through Jesus' sacrifice. All it takes is for you to say "Yes, I believe in Jesus and in what He did for me. I believe that Jesus is God who came in the flesh and died for my sins and took my full punishment on the cross of Calvary so that my sins are forgiven and my punishment due to me already paid for by Jesus Himself". This was and is God's pleasure and will for your life. This is what He chose for you. When you say "Yes" to Jesus and receive His Life for your life, you belong to the family of God.

> *"For God so loved the world that he gave his one and only Son, that whoever believes in him shall not perish but have eternal life" (John 3:16, emphasis added).*

God the Father loved you so much that He gave His one and only Son (Jesus) to die on a Cross so that He could have a relationship with you. Because of your sin, He could not have a relationship with you. The only way He could have a relationship with you is for Him to sacrifice His one and only Son so that your sins could be forgiven. It caused God the Father great emotional pain to sacrifice His only Son BUT He did it so that He could have a relationship with YOU. He loves you this much.

> *"May the grace of the Lord Jesus Christ, and the love of God, and the fellowship of the Holy Spirit be with you all" (2 Corinthians 13:14, emphasis added).*

God loves you so much that He sent His Holy Spirit to be with you at all times. God says that He will never leave you nor forsake you. You are not alone. His Spirit is with you always. In fact, as a believer, His Spirit lives in you. You cannot be separated from God because His Spirit lives in you. You can fellowship with Holy Spirit at any time. You can talk to Him. He will direct you, teach you, comfort you, love you, empower you, help you, gift you, etc. God's Spirit living in you is another part of your inheritance in Christ

Jesus. Acknowledge Him in your everyday life. He is part of God. Remember that God is a three part being (God the Father, God the Son and God the Holy Spirit). If you look at this scripture again, you will see all three parts of the Godhead.

> *"May Christ through your faith [actually] dwell – settle down, abide, make His permanent home – in your hearts! May you be rooted deep in **love** and founded securely on **love**, That you may have the power and be strong to apprehend and **grasp** with all the saints (God's devoted people, the experience of that **love**) what is the breadth and length and height and depth [of it]; {That you may really come} to know – practically, through experience for yourselves – the **love of Christ**, which far surpasses mere knowledge (without experience); that you may be filled (through all your being) unto all the fullness of God – [that is] may have the richest measure of the divine Presence, and become a body wholly filled and flooded with God Himself!" (Ephesians 3:17-19, Amplified, emphasis added)*

The word "grasp" in this scripture means to grab hold of firmly. God wants you to firmly grab hold of His love for you. God wants to fill you with His love to overflowing. In fact, He wants to fill you with Himself. That's what this scripture says. He wants you to experience the full measure of His love. Why? Because it is God's Will for you to be made whole in every area of your life. When you are filled with God's love, nothing will be able to separate you from Him. He wants to spend every second with you in this life and for all eternity. He loves you that much.

> *"But when the kindness and love of God our Savior appeared, he saved us, not because of righteous things we had done, but because of his mercy" (Titus 3:4-5).*

Can you see from this scripture that God loves you unconditionally? His love is not contingent upon you doing good things or doing everything right. He loves you even when you do things wrong. He loves you even when you make mistakes. He is a merciful God.

There's a scripture that says God's mercies are new every morning (see Lamentations 3:22-23 in the KJV). Receive His mercies every morning for your day. I have made a habit of doing this. This is a good habit to form. I pray that God will remind you of this every morning when you wake up.

Prayer: Father, in Jesus' Name, fill me with Yourself so that I will overflow with Your love. Please turn my thinking (my believing) right side up, where it is upside down. Help me to renew my mind with Your Word so that I will know who I am in Christ and know Your perfect will and plan for my life. Thank you Father that I am chosen by You and adopted into Your family. You delight in me. I am special to You. I am the apple of Your eye. I am valued by You. I am Your treasure. I am important to You. You care about me. You love me unconditionally. I receive Your forgiveness for my sins. I receive Your unconditional love for me. Every morning help me to receive Your mercies for that day.

"How great is the love the Father has lavished on us,
that we should be called children of God!" (1 John 3:1)

The word "lavish" in the Webster's dictionary means: very generous, very abundant, to give or spend generously. God is very generous with His love. He is not stingy with His love. He pours out His love into your heart in abundance. He lavishes His love on you because you belong to Him as His child.

"In your unfailing love you will lead the people you
have redeemed. In your strength you will guide them
to your holy mountain" (Exodus 15:13).

In this scripture, "holy mountain" is symbolic of God's Presence. It says that He leads us by His unfailing love into His Presence. When we know the love of God for us personally, we will run into His

Presence because we know that we are accepted by Him. He will not reject us because of His great love for us. When we are filled with His love, we will experience His manifested Presence in our lives. There is nothing sweeter than being in His manifested Presence. If you desire to be in His manifested Presence, let Him know.

"The Lord is slow to anger, abounding in love and forgiving sin and rebellion" (Numbers 14:18a).

God is not a harsh judge. He is a loving Father who cares more deeply about His creation than we can even imagine. His love abounds which means His love is plentiful. He overflows with love. He is slow to anger which means He patiently waits and gives us opportunities to repent and turn to Him. If you are a child of God and you want to live right before God but you are struggling in some areas to get the victory, no matter what sin you have committed God's love and forgiveness covers it. Don't let the guilt, condemnation and shame of your sins keep you from running to God. The enemy plans to load you down with guilt, condemnation and shame to keep you away from God. In all your failures run to Him and receive His forgiveness. Know that He has already forgiven you in Christ Jesus who died for you and who bore all your punishment at the cross. Stop punishing yourself and run to your blessed Savior who can free you from that sin whatever it is. Receive His grace and His free gift of righteousness and you will reign over that sin for it shall not have dominion over you (see Romans 5:17b). You are in Jesus and Jesus is in you. Therefore, no sin can continue to have power over you. Renew your mind with the Word of God and start being righteous conscious instead of sin conscious. When you are sin conscious, you are giving power to the sin in your life BUT when you are righteous conscious, you are allowing God's power in you to overcome that sin in your life and to live a life of victory. If you are stuck in a sin, allow God to set you free from it. You may not be completely free overnight but stick with God and allow Him to help you be righteous conscious. Get your mind renewed with the Word of God so that you will see yourself the way He sees you and you will walk in victory.

"Your love, O Lord, reaches to the heavens, your faithfulness to the skies" (Psalm 36:5).

Can God's love for you be measured? This scripture says God's love reaches to the heavens. When I think of the heavens I think of the galaxies and the space beyond and I realize that this distance cannot be measured. Therefore, God's love cannot be measured. It is endless.

Whatever it is you need to be free from, declare that God's love is greater. Declare it now.

"[For my concern is} that their hearts may be braced (comforted, cheered and encouraged) as they are knit together in love, that they may come to have all the abounding wealth and blessings of assured conviction of understanding, and that they may become progressively more intimately acquainted with, and may know more definitely and accurately and thoroughly, that mystic secret of God [which is] Christ, the Anointed One" (Colossians 2:2-4, Amplified).

Wow! Can we really know God's love for us like this? Can we really know the abounding wealth and blessings and have assured conviction that we are loved? Can we really become progressively more intimately acquainted with and may know more definitely and accurately and thoroughly God's love for us? The Bible says we can and it comes through knowing and experiencing Jesus Christ. We will experience His love as we mediate on what Jesus did for us on the cross and as we meditate on scriptures like the ones we have been reading in this Chapter.

*"And this is my prayer: **that your love may abound more and more in knowledge and depth of insight**, so that you may be able to discern what is best and may be pure and blameless until the day of Christ" (Philippians 1:9-10, emphasis added).*

Paul's prayer for the Church was that the Church, God's children, would understand and know the love of God for them personally and that the Church would know God's love more and more, day after day until Jesus returns for His Church.

God's love is part of our inheritance in Christ Jesus.

I would encourage you to find scriptures on God's love for you and to meditate on these scriptures until you know that He loves you unconditionally and completely. You can look up the word "love" in a concordance and find scriptures on love. You can write down these scriptures and then write down what these scriptures are saying to you personally. This will help you to meditate on them and get the truth of God's Word in your heart so that you will believe that God loves YOU.

Prayer: Father, in Jesus' Name, thank You that I belong to You. I belong to Your family. I am accepted by You, just the way I am. I receive Your measureless love for me, and Your acceptance of me, just the way I am. Please guide me by Your unfailing love into Your Presence so that I may experience You in real and personal ways more and more until Jesus returns for me.

Now you need to continue to think in line with the Word of God that He loves you. Bring into captivity every wrong thought that exalts itself above the Word of God. Ignore those wrong thoughts and speak forth what God says about you. That you are greatly loved, that you are forgiven, that you are the righteousness of God in Christ Jesus, that you are blessed in Jesus, that you are the head and not the tail and that you are victorious in Christ Jesus.

You see the enemy of your soul wants you to think that you are defeated, that God is angry with you and that you are a failure and will never amount to anything. Don't give any place to these wrong thoughts anymore. They come from the enemy. Listen to what God says about you. Believe that He loves you.

Receiving Your Inheritance
In Jesus Christ Brings Joy

*D*id you know that the New Covenant is the New Testament in the Bible? A lot of people will go to a lawyer and have their Last Will and Testament prepared so that they can sign it. They instruct their lawyer what to put in their Last Will and Testament, who they want as their Executor and Trustee of their Estate and who their beneficiaries will be. When they die, they trust their Executor and Trustee to properly administer their Estate and distribute their assets to their beneficiaries in accordance with their Last Will and Testament.

Jesus' Spirit instructed a number of people to write the New Testament (His Last Will and Testament). Some of those who He instructed to write the New Testament are Matthew, Mark, Luke, John, Paul, Peter and Timothy. Jesus' Spirit gave them His instructions on what He wanted in His Last Will and Testament.

I heard a story about a blind woman who had taken care of a man for many years and just prior to his death, he gave this woman a piece of paper. After this man died, since this woman could not see and did not know what this piece of paper was, she framed it as it was the only thing he left her. The man that died was a very wealthy man. The blind woman was very poor and after this man's death she continued to live in abject poverty only to discover one day near the end of her life that the piece of paper that the man had given to her was his Last Will and Testament and he named her as his sole beneficiary.

Let us not be like this woman who had this man's whole estate and did not know what she had.

Unless we get understanding of what is in the Last Will and Testament of Jesus Christ, we will not be able to partake of and receive the inheritance that He left to us, His bride. So let's now look at what our inheritance is in Christ Jesus. As we come into the understanding of what Jesus has willed to us, let us receive it and partake of it with joy for our everyday living.

Prayer: Father, in Jesus' Name, thank you for enlightening the eyes of my heart as I look at what Jesus has given to me in His Last Will and Testament. Help me to grab hold of it firmly, to receive it and partake of it every day with joy throughout my life.

I have already mentioned to you some things that are part of our inheritance in Christ Jesus i.e. God's love for us personally, God's rest from our self-efforts, hope, protection, stability during emotional times, healing, deliverance, comfort, forgiveness of sins, freedom, compassion, satisfaction in Jesus and renewed youth. This is quite a list already but there is so much more.

Let's delve in even further into the Last Will and Testament of Jesus Christ to find out more of what our inheritance is. Pay close attention as you will want to remember what your inheritance is so that you can partake of it daily.

1. Salvation and Intimacy with Jesus

First and foremost our inheritance is Jesus Himself, our Bridegroom, and everything that is His. We get the **whole package**. Jesus alone is more than enough but because of His great love for us He gives us everything that belongs to Him.

> *"Then I saw a new heaven and a new earth, for the first heaven and the first earth had passed away, and there was no longer any sea. I saw the Holy City, the **New Jerusalem**, coming down out of heaven from God, prepared **as a bride** beautifully dressed for her husband (the New Jerusalem, the Holy City is us; we are the bride of Christ; we are the New Jerusalem).*

*And I heard a loud voice from the throne saying, "Now the dwelling of God is with men, and he will live with them. They will be his people, and God himself will be with them and be their God. He will wipe every tear from their eyes. There will be no more death or mourning or crying or pain, for the old order of things has passed away." He who was seated on the throne said, "I am making everything new!" Then he said, "Write this down, for these words are trustworthy and true." He said to me: "It is done. I am the Alpha and the Omega, the Beginning and the End. To him who is thirsty I will give to drink without cost from the spring of the water of life. He who overcomes **will inherit all this**, and I will be his God and he will be my son" (Revelation 21:1-7, emphasis and parenthesis added).*

Jesus has given us salvation as our inheritance. Salvation and a life with God Himself now and for all eternity is the **greatest inheritance** one could ever receive. Our inheritance begins at the moment of salvation not when we get to heaven. We are His Bride now and forever as long as we continue to believe in Him. Jesus has given us an inheritance even now in this life on earth to partake of. As we journey through this life we journey knowing that God is always with us and that He will never leave us nor forsake us. He has promised us this in His Word.

2. Spirit of wisdom & revelation and Spiritual enlightenment

*"I keep asking that the God of our Lord Jesus Christ, the glorious Father, may give you the **Spirit of wisdom and revelation**, so that you may know him better. I pray also that the **eyes of your heart may be enlightened** in order that you may know the hope to which he has called you, the riches of his glorious inheritance in the saints, and his incomparably great power for us who believe" (Ephesians 1:17-19a, emphasis added).*

51

These verses are packed with riches from heaven. First of all, Jesus has given us the Spirit of wisdom and revelation as our inheritance. We only need to thank Him for it and receive it. Why does He give this to us? It says, so that we may know Him better. When we know Him better, we will discover even more riches that we can partake of.

Also, verse 18 refers to **the eyes of our heart being enlightened** but we must know that this is our inheritance and receive it in order to benefit from it. When the eyes of our heart are enlightened, we will understand things we did not understand before. Things that our heart was blinded to before, we will now understand and see with our spiritual eyes. Why does God want us to see with the eyes of our heart? Paul goes on to tell us. He says in order that we may know:

- **The hope** to which God has called us,
- The **riches of His glorious inheritance** in the saints, and
- His **incomparably great power** for us who believe.

Prayer: Father, in Jesus' Name, I receive the Spirit of wisdom and revelation to know You better. I thank you for enlightening the eyes of my heart. I thank you for giving me understanding of things I have not understood before as this is my inheritance in Christ Jesus.

3. Fruit of righteousness

> *"And this is my prayer: that your love may abound more and more in knowledge and depth of insight, so that you may be able to discern what is best and may be pure and blameless until the day of Christ, filled with the **fruit** of **righteousness** that comes through Jesus Christ – to the glory and praise of God"* (Philippians 1:9-11, emphasis added).

I asked the Holy Spirit to tell me what the fruit of righteousness is and He immediately brought to my mind the fruit of the Spirit. Let's look at that scripture.

> *"But the fruit of the Spirit is love, joy, peace, patience, kindness, goodness, faithfulness, gentleness and self-control" (Galatians 5:22-23a).*

I have lived most of my Christian life trying to **develop** the fruit of the Spirit by working with all my efforts to walk in this fruit. I have come to understand that this is my inheritance and Jesus has freely given this fruit to me by giving me His Spirit. I am filled with the Holy Spirit and, therefore, I am also filled with His fruit. They come with His Spirit who lives in me. As a believer in Jesus, I have them now. What I need to do is partake of them and receive them, use them in my everyday life, wear them just like I would wear a beautiful ring that someone bequeathed to me. I would wear it with joy. I can wear the fruit of the Spirit with joy. I can let the fruit of the Spirit flow through me. It is there already in my life. All I need to do is partake of this inheritance that is already mine.

The verse above says "filled with the **fruit of righteousness** that comes through Jesus Christ". The Holy Spirit showed me that to be filled with the fruit of righteousness (these 9 fruits), I need to know and understand and believe that I am the righteousness of God in Christ Jesus. Unless I know this, I will not be able to partake of the 9 fruits of the Spirit. When I believe that I am righteous simply because I believe in Jesus and in His finished work on the cross, I will confidently partake of the fruit of the Spirit that already lives in me. The more I believe that I am as righteous as Jesus is because He gave me His righteousness (I did not earn it and, in fact, I cannot earn it), the more I will walk in the fruit of the Spirit. The more I freely receive His righteousness, the more I will walk in **His** love, the more I will walk in **His** joy, the more I will walk in **His** peace, etc. This is my inheritance. All I need to do is believe it belongs to me and receive it.

Please **stop trying to develop** the fruit and **start believing** that you have been made righteous. Become aware that the fruit of the Spirit is in you. Draw on that fruit and it will begin to flow out from the inside of you.

4. Holy Spirit and His Gifts

*"There are different kinds of gifts, but the **same Spirit**.
There are different kinds of service, but the **same Lord**.
There are different kinds of working, but the **same
God** works all of them in all men. Now to each one the
manifestation of the Spirit is given for the common
good. To one there is given through the Spirit the message of wisdom; to another the message of knowledge by means of the **same Spirit**, to another faith
by the **same Spirit**, to another gifts of healing by that
one Spirit, to another miraculous powers to another
prophecy, to another distinguishing between spirits,
to another speaking in different kinds of tongues,
and to still another the interpretation of tongues. All
these are the work of one and the **same Spirit**, and
he gives them to each one, just as he determines"* (1
Corinthians 12:4-11, emphasis added).

Did you see that it is the manifestation of the Spirit that is freely
given for the common good of mankind? (The word "manifest"
means apparent to the senses or the mind, obvious, to show plainly,
reveal.) The gifts are given for the common good of mankind **so that**
the Spirit of God would be revealed, plainly seen and made obvious
to the people He wants to minister to through us. Spiritual gifts are
given as a result of God's grace and are not the result of human effort
or merit. We cannot merit the gifts of the Holy Spirit. The Holy
Spirit is our inheritance from who will flow His gifts. Don't desire
the gifts without first recognizing the Holy Spirit and giving Him
preeminence. It is the Holy Spirit who lives in us and who operates
His gifts through us. Without Him in our lives, there will be no gifts
flowing from us. It is His wisdom, His faith, His healing, etc. operating through us. The Bible tells us to follow the way of love and
eagerly desire spiritual gifts, especially the gift of prophesy (see 1
Corinthians 14:1). The Holy Spirit gives gifts to reveal Himself to
us and others. He makes Himself obvious to us. He shows Himself
plainly to us and others. He makes Himself apparent to our senses.

We sense His manifested presence in our lives. For example, when the Holy Spirit gives us a word of knowledge or a prophesy for someone, it is to make Himself known to that person.

Jesus gave us His Spirit. He bequeathed to us His very own Spirit. He said unless I go, I cannot send my Spirit to you. **His Spirit is His very own life**. Have you ever thought of that before? To have Jesus is to have His Spirit (His life). They are the same. Jesus died so that He could give us His life (His Spirit) as our inheritance. John 10:10(b) says that I have come to give you life and to give you life more abundantly. We have inherited Jesus' life (His Spirit). He freely gives us His Spirit (His life) and from His Spirit will flow wisdom, knowledge, faith, healing, miraculous powers, prophecy, discernment, tongues and interpretation of tongues. As we recognize who the Holy Spirit is and give Him room to move in our lives, His gifts will automatically flow through us so that He will be revealed, plainly seen and made known to others.

5. Armor of God

*"Finally, be strong in the Lord and in his mighty power. **Put on** the full armor of God so that you can **take** your stand against the devil's schemes" (Ephesians 6:10-11, emphasis added).*

*"Therefore, **put on** the full armor of God, so that when the day of evil comes, you may be able to stand your ground and after you have done everything to stand. Stand firm then, with the belt of truth buckled around your waist, with the breastplate of righteousness in place, and with your feet fitted with the readiness that comes from the gospel of peace. In addition to all this, **take up** the shield of faith, with which you can extinguish all the flaming arrows of the evil one. **Take** the helmet of salvation and the sword of the Spirit, which is the word of God. And pray in the Spirit on all occasions with all kinds of prayers and requests. With this*

in mind, be alert and always keep on praying for all
the saints" (Ephesians 6:13-18, emphasis added).

In verse 13 the NIV says to **put on** the full armor of God. The KJV says in verse 13 to **take unto you** the whole armor of God.

I looked up the word "take" in the Strong's Exhaustive Concordance and it means to receive up, take in, take unto and take up.

To take something is to receive it. In other words, to put on the armor of God is to take it unto yourself and receive it. Putting on the armor of God is not something we do **externally.** In other words, we are not clothed with God's armor by simply saying "I put on the helmet of salvation, the belt of truth, etc." Being clothed with the armor of God is to be clothed with the Lord Jesus Christ Himself from the **inside out.** It is when we get the truth of God's Word into our hearts and coming out of our mouths that we are truly clothed with God's armor.

God tells us that His armor is necessary to stand against the enemy's schemes. He says that we are to be strong **in Him** and **in His mighty power** not in our own power. We are in a spiritual war, but we do not have to defeat the enemy because Jesus has already defeated him. However, we do need to receive by faith what grace has already made available to us so that it will be manifested in our lives. We do have to stand our ground and not allow our enemy to bully us into thinking that we are defeated. How do we do this? The only way we can stand against his schemes is to be fully clothed (arrayed) with the armor of God.

Jesus has bequeathed His armor to us. This is exciting and very good news. Each piece of the armor of God is exactly what it is. It is **God's armor** that we **take** unto ourselves and **receive** so that we can stand firm against the enemy. Each piece of the armor is so closely intertwined because **each piece is a part of Jesus Himself.** It is not an external clothing but one that takes place on the inside of us as we begin to understand and receive revelation of what each piece of the armor of God is to us. It is spiritual armor. We simply need to understand what we have as a child of God so that we can walk fully clothed with Jesus Himself.

So, what are the pieces of the Armor of God and how do we take them up so that we are clothed with Jesus Himself from the inside out?

a. Truth

Jesus is the way, the truth and the life (see John 14:6).

We can stand our ground against the enemy by knowing and receiving Truth. Jesus is Truth. Jesus is the embodiment of Truth. Jesus lives in us. Almighty God lives in us. Truth lives in us because Jesus is Truth and He lives in us.

As a believer, how do we take unto ourselves Truth?

Putting on the Belt of Truth is getting to know Jesus personally and intimately by renewing our minds with Truth, which is His Word. We put His Word into our hearts. The Bible says that the Truth shall set us free. It is when we receive on the inside of us a revelation of Truth (who Jesus is to us personally) that we are clothed with this piece of the armor. You are being clothed as you receive the Truth in this Book.

Truth will break, destroy and free us from yokes of bondage. If we find ourselves in a situation (e.g. sorrow, sickness, poverty, depression, confusion, fear, condemnation, lack, etc.) find out what God's Word says about it and then hold on to Truth. Receive God's promises the same way you received salvation: by grace through faith in Jesus. Romans 10:9 says "That if you confess with your mouth, Jesus is Lord, and believe in your heart that God raised him from the dead you will be saved". If we confess with our mouth God's precious promises and believe them with our heart, we will have them. We hold on to God's Promises by meditating on (thinking about and speaking out) God's Word (Truth) pertaining to our situation and thanking God for His specific Promises.

b. Righteousness

Jesus is righteous and **He** is our righteousness (see Jeremiah 23:6).

Through Adam we were all born sinners, but through Jesus we were **made** righteous. Jesus made us righteous by giving us His righteousness. We are not **being made** righteous. We are righteous now because we have been given Jesus' righteousness. I am in Jesus and He made me righteous. I need to take unto myself and receive His righteousness. I need to believe that I am the righteousness of God in Christ Jesus and that His righteousness is inside of me. This is so very important for us, as believers, to understand and grab hold of. It is a weapon that we use to stand firm against the enemy when he comes to try to lie and deceive us.

> *"not having a righteousness of my own that comes from the law, but that which is through **faith in Christ** – the righteousness that comes from God and is **by faith**" (Philippians 3:9, emphasis added).*

We receive righteousness **by faith**. We simply believe that Jesus gave us His righteousness. We simply receive it **by faith**. We may not feel righteous but it is **by faith** that we are the righteousness of God in Christ Jesus.

The scriptures refer to two kinds of righteousness. There is a self-righteousness and there is a righteousness that comes by faith. A self-righteous person thinks they are better than others. They tell people to live one way while they live another way. They do things for recognition (to be noticed by people). Their heart motivations are wrong. We can be self-righteous if we think we can get to heaven by simply being a good person and by doing good works. We can be self-righteous by thinking that we will become more righteous by our own efforts. This actually means that we are good enough to make it to heaven by our own efforts of goodness, rather than by accepting what Jesus did for us on the cross. This way of thinking actually is implying that Jesus died on the cross for nothing.

When we are self-righteous, we think we have this breastplate of righteousness in place when we really don't. We think we are protected by this piece of the armor, but we really aren't.

Once we are born again, we need to understand that Jesus has put us into a right standing with our Heavenly Father. We are no longer separated spiritually from God. We are as righteous as Jesus is because Jesus has clothed us with His righteousness from the inside out.

c. Peace

Jesus is Peace. He is our Prince of Peace.

We are to fit our **feet** with the readiness that comes from the Gospel of Peace. What does this mean?

> *"You will go out in joy and **be led forth in peace**; the mountains and hills will burst into song before you, and all the trees of the field will clap their hands" (Isaiah 55:12, emphasis added).*

I believe "feet" symbolizes us moving forward in our walk with God. God wants us to be led, or to move forward, by His peace. He wants us to make decisions from a peaceful mind and heart and not from an anxious mind or out of anxious emotions. As we are led by peace, we will make right choices and right decisions. When we move out of God's Will, we will experience a lack of peace.

How do we keep peace in our lives?

> *"You will keep in perfect peace him whose mind is steadfast, because he trusts in you" (Isaiah 26:3).*

KJV says "whose mind is stayed on thee".

This scripture tells us to keep our minds focused on God and He will keep us in perfect peace. Simply trust Him and He will do the rest.

> *"Do not be anxious about anything, but in everything, by prayer and petition, with thanksgiving, present your requests to God. And the **peace of God**, which transcends all understanding, will guard your hearts and your minds in Christ Jesus" (Philippians 4:6-7, emphasis added).*

This scripture says we are to cast our cares upon the Lord. Cast all your anxiety, worry, fears (this includes sorrows) upon the Lord. Pray about things that are bothering you and put them in God's hands and He will give you peace.

I want to mention something here that the Holy Spirit has showed me about my own life. Sometimes I would get so excited about what God was doing and how He was answering prayers that I could not settle my mind down to sleep at night. I allowed myself to get over excited. The Lord showed me that I even needed to cast all my excitement upon Him so that it would not keep me awake at night. If you are an excitable person, cast this excitement upon the Lord early in the evening. Ask the Holy Spirit to help you do this so that you can sleep peacefully at night.

> *"Peace I leave with you; my peace I give you. I do not give to you as the world gives. Do not let your hearts be troubled and do not be afraid" (John 14:27).*

The word "peace" in this scripture is the word "shalom" in Hebrew. In addition to meaning peace, calm and quietness of heart, mind and emotions, it also means wellness (health), prosperity, rest, safety, welfare, wholeness and completeness. It denotes a state of untroubled, undisturbed wellbeing. This is the peace that Jesus gives to us.

Jesus gives us His very own peace. He gives us the peace He enjoyed while on earth. He gives us everlasting peace. He does not give as the world gives. The world gives and takes away but Jesus only gives. He will not take His peace from us. However, we are not to let our hearts be troubled and afraid which will rob us of peace. We need to let go of the things in our lives that our troubling us and depend on God to take care of the situation i.e. children, finances, jobs, ill health, etc. We do this by keeping our eyes on Jesus and declaring His promises over our situation. (see Chapter "Walking on Water")

> *"Cast all your anxiety on him because he cares for you" (1 Peter 5:7).*

It is God's Word, the Gospel of Peace, that we take and receive into our hearts that will bring us peace.

There is one further thing I would like to mention regarding this piece of armor. Peace that takes place on the inside of us will cause us to stand firm and hold our ground against the enemy. It will cause us to be resolute like David who ran towards Goliath (the giant in his life) with his trust in God alone. David did not wait for Goliath to come after him. David ran towards Goliath trusting in God to defeat him because David knew his God. He came against Goliath in the name of the Lord Almighty, the God of the armies of Israel and he declared that the Lord would hand Goliath over to him and the whole world would know that there is a God in Israel (see 1 Samuel 17:45-46). Now that Jesus has defeated the enemy for us, we can use our feet to trample upon our Goliath for he is under **our feet**. We are the head and not the tail, the top and not the bottom (see Deuteronomy 28:13). When we are firmly established in the Gospel of Peace, we will trample upon our enemy by declaring God's Word and His Promises in every circumstance in our lives.

d. Faith

Jesus is our faith.

We live by the faith of the Son of God. We live by His faith.
Are you starting to see that these pieces of the armor are all about who Jesus is to us as children of God? He is Truth. He is our righteousness. He is our peace. He is our faith.

> *"By faith in the name of Jesus, this man whom you see and know was made strong. It is Jesus' name **and the faith that comes through him** that has given this complete healing to him, as you can all see" (Acts 3:16, emphasis added).*

The Armor is for us to stand our ground against the enemy. Jesus already defeated him but we have to use faith to believe that he is already defeated. When we believe he is defeated, we will be able to stand against him. **It's not faith in our ability to stand against him but faith in Jesus who is our faith**. Our faith is in Him not in ourselves. I have faith in the fact that God is faithful even when I'm not faithful.

> *"I am crucified with Christ: nevertheless I live; yet not I, but Christ liveth in me: and the life which I now live in the flesh I live by the **faith of the Son of God**, who loved me, and gave himself for me" (Galatians 2:20, KJV, emphasis added).*

Did you see that? I now live by the faith of the Son of God. As I get God's Word into my heart, I will have His faith living on the inside of me.

Our faith should not be in what we can do. Our faith should be in Jesus and in what He has already done for us on the cross. He did it all. When He said on the cross "It is finished" He had already made available to us every provision that we will ever need. We just need to take in and receive it.

Verse 16 says to take up the shield of faith. How do we do that? **We receive His faith to believe His promises**. Now in order to believe His promises, we need to know what His precious promises are. As we read the Word of God, we will discover more of Jesus and His Promises for us. He gave us His promises so that we will receive them and take them unto ourselves. They are free. We don't have to become a Bible scholar but as we take in God's Word and get to know Him the way He really is, our faith in Jesus and in what He has already done for us will grow. This will cause His faith that is already in our spirit to arise within our soul. A spiritual shield of faith will arise from the inside of us.

> *"If you have faith as small as a mustard seed, you can say to this mulberry tree, be up-rooted and planted in the sea, and it will obey you" (Luke 17:6).*

Think about that. A tree obeying us, yet God's Word says it will. A mustard seed is a very small seed, but when it is planted and watered properly it will grow into a very large tree. I believe God is saying that we don't have to wait until our faith is perfected to be able to receive what we ask for. Even when our faith is only the size of a mustard seed, it is powerful enough to receive from God. However, it can become even more powerful as we receive more and more revelation from God's Word.

I have seen pictures of very large trees after a hurricane has uprooted them and turned them over on their side. It is an eye-opener to see the power behind a hurricane and what it can destroy in such a short period of time. God's Word says in the above scripture that if we have faith as small as a mustard seed, it will be as powerful as uprooting a tree and planting it in the sea. The pictures I saw only showed the hurricane having turned the trees on their side. This scripture says that our faith, even in the beginning stages of its growth, can actually move trees from one place to another. Of course, God is giving an analogy of what faith can accomplish. We may never use our faith to move a tree, but we can use our faith to stand against the enemy of sorrow, sickness, lack, destruction, etc. and move these things out of our lives. We can also use our faith to trust God to draw us closer to Him, to give us the desire for His Word, to pray through us when we don't know how to pray, to help us surrender to Him as the Lord of our lives, to help us to be led by the Holy Spirit, to give us wisdom in every circumstance that we find ourselves in, etc. When we use our faith, we will stand our ground against our enemy.

e. Salvation

Jesus is our Savior

Verse 17a says to take the helmet of salvation.

We see two key words here: "Helmet" and "Salvation".

Helmet means encirclement of the head. A helmet is something that is placed on one's head. The helmet of salvation is placed on our head to protect our mind and thoughts from the lies and deception of the enemy. This takes place on the inside of us as we renew our minds with the Word of God. When the enemy tries to attack our mind and thoughts with lies, such as, that we are not saved, points out all of our faults to condemn us, tells us that we will never make it or amount to anything, etc., we can look to God's Word and receive, believe and speak out the Truth about ourselves.

> *"Do not conform any longer to the pattern of this world, but be transformed by the **renewing of your mind**. Then you will be able to test and approve what God's will is – his good, pleasing and perfect will"* *(Romans 12:2, emphasis added).*

There is a battle in our minds. The enemy tries to bombard us with thoughts of sorrow, fear, condemnation, lack, death and lies to keep us in bondage to him. However, when our minds are renewed with the Word of God, we will not listen to the enemy's lies but rather we will boldly declare God's Word over our lives and our situations. **The understanding of God's Word is the greatest defense against the lies of the enemy.**

Salvation is translated "soteria" in the Greek and means saving as well as deliverance, health and wholeness. Yes, wholeness. Often we only look at salvation as being saved and going to heaven. Although that in itself is wonderful, it means far more than that. It also means deliverance, health and wholeness including prosperity in every area of our lives (our physical and mental health, our finances, our marriages, our homes, our relationships, our careers, etc.) All this is part of our inheritance in Christ Jesus.

Believe, receive and take up the helmet of salvation and everything it comprises.

f. Sword of the Spirit

Jesus is our sword.

A sword is something we use against an enemy. Verse 17b says that the sword of the Spirit is the **Word of God**. John 1:1 says that Jesus is the Word of God. Therefore, Jesus is the sword of the Spirit. How do we take up the sword of the Spirit? We take up the sword of the Spirit by speaking **God's Word** with our mouth. Since this weapon is to be used against the enemy, we cannot just think it in our mind because the devil cannot read our mind. We have to speak it out loud as that's when it becomes a sword.

In Revelation 1:16 where it describes Jesus in all His glory, it says that out of **His mouth** came a sharp double-edged sword.

It came out of His mouth. The sword (Jesus) needs to come out of our mouth too.

> *"For the **word of God** is living and active. Sharper than any double-edged sword" (Hebrew 4:12a, emphasis added).*

In the natural, if someone came at you with a sword and was prepared to use it and you did not have any defense against that sword, you would turn around as fast as you could and take off. The same is true when we use our sword against the enemy. He takes off as fast as he can. He knows he has no defense against the sword, which is the **Word of God**.

Jesus used the sword of the Spirit at the end of His 40 days in the desert when the devil was promising Him things. Let's read that scripture.

> *"All this I will give you", he said, "if you will bow down and worship me." **Jesus said** to him, "Away from me, Satan! For it is written: Worship the Lord your God, and serve him only" (Matthew 4:9-10, emphasis added).*

Jesus took authority over satan when He told him to leave. Then He quoted scripture.

The following is an example of how to take authority over sorrow in your life.

In the Name of Jesus, I take authority over sorrow, sadness, despair and every like thing. I command you to leave me and to go where Jesus is telling you to go. Don't ever come back to me or transfer to anyone else. Jesus I thank You that you came to set me free from sorrow, grief and despair. Your Word says in Isaiah 61 that you came to comfort all who mourn, to give us a crown of beauty instead of ashes, the oil of gladness instead of mourning and a garment of praise instead of a spirit of despair. I receive freedom right now Jesus from these things and I receive Your comfort, goodness, oil of gladness and a garment to praise You. Thank You Jesus for setting me free. Whom the Son sets free is free in deed.

Did you notice that I took authority and then quoted scripture?

This is how we take up the sword of the Spirit. Just like Jesus used His authority and then quoted scripture to defeat the enemy, we take authority and quote scripture to defeat the enemy in our lives.

Whatever it is that you need to take authority over, find out what God's Word says about it and take up your sword. Speak to that mountain and command it to leave you and then quote His Word and you will stand against the attacks of the enemy in your life.

g. Pray in the Spirit

This piece of the armor is the key to all of the other pieces.

I believe God intended that praying in the Spirit is also a piece of the armor of God. In the New International Version the word "and" links praying in the Spirit with the other pieces of the armor. The other pieces of the armor all refer to Jesus. Jesus is Truth, He is Righteous, He is Peace, He is our Faith, He is our Savior and He is the Sword of the Spirit. This 7th piece of the armor is referring to the Holy Spirit. Keep in mind here, that the Holy Spirit **is** the Spirit of our Heavenly Father and the Spirit of Jesus. All three are one.

Praying reminds us that the battle of faith is spiritual and must be fought in prayer first. Without prayer, we will not be enlightened when we hear or read the Word of God and, therefore, we will not be able to take up and receive the armor of God. Without prayer, we will not be able to stand against the attacks of the enemy. When you pray, always pray from a place of victory and not defeat. When you pray, always believe. If you are having difficulty believing that God will answer your prayers, ask Him to help you to believe. I've done this many times.

Throughout this Book I have included prayers for you to pray. As you pray them, you are taking unto yourself this piece of the Armor.

This scripture tells us that we are to pray on **all** occasions. In order to pray on all occasions, we need to realize that prayer is a way of life. We can be praying as we are on the go. Prayer is talking to God throughout the day. Yes, it is good to set specific times to devote to prayer but prayer doesn't end there. As we go throughout our day with a heart of thanksgiving and praise, we are praying. Praying is communicating with God. Even asking and consulting Him in situations we find ourselves in when we don't know what to do throughout the day, is prayer. For example, at work if you are faced with a difficult job, ask God for wisdom and His direction. This is prayer. If you can't find your keys, ask God where they are. This is prayer. It is a continual communication with God. Prayer is being God conscious. It is when we have God on our minds and we are conscious of His Presence in our lives. Prayer is depending on God and knowing that He is there for you. In other words, throughout the day, we talk to God about everything. We communicate with Him spirit to spirit all day long. **Prayer is a relationship with a personal God**.

If you don't know how to pray about a certain situation in your life, ask the Holy Spirit to pray through you. Then pray in the Spirit with your prayer language until something comes to your mind to pray. Let Him take over your prayer life. Let the Holy Spirit be in charge. Let the Holy Spirit take His rightful place in your life and in your prayers. He is available to us at all times to intercede through us if we will give room to Him.

> *"The prayer of a righteous man is powerful and effective" (James 5:16b).*

If we are born again, we are righteous because Jesus has given us His righteousness and our prayers are powerful and effective.

Pray the Word. God watches over His Word to bring it to pass in our lives.

Each piece of the armor is so closely intertwined because each piece is a part of Jesus Himself. As we fix our eyes on Him, the **Word of God**, and get to know and receive and take Him into our hearts more and more through the **Word** we will begin to understand that He is Truth, that He is our Righteousness, that He is our Prince of

Peace, that He is our Faith, that He is our Salvation, that He is the Sword of the Spirit and that He gave us **His** Spirit who intercedes through us enabling us to pray about everything as we yield ourselves to Him. Did you see that the Armor of God is all about Jesus and getting to know Him better through the Word of God?

As we put God's Word into our hearts day by day, little by little, we become the **warrior** that God intends for us to be and we are fully clothed with Jesus Himself from the inside out. His armor begins on the inside of us. He becomes so big on the inside of us that we emulate Him. When we are so filled with Jesus Himself, people will look at us and they will see Jesus. When the enemy looks at us, he will see Jesus. That's being clothed with His Armor.

Can you see just how important it is for us to **know** Jesus, who is the Word of God? The Word of God is our inheritance that enables us to stand our ground against the devil's schemes.

Why don't you pray right now that God will give you a hunger and a thirst for His Word. **His Word is your inheritance and it becomes your Armor when you get it inside of you.** He wants you to know His Word so that you can take your stand and walk in victory.

6. Baptism of the Holy Spirit

If you are already baptized in the Holy Spirit, please do not skip this section as it also reveals the importance and benefits of being baptized.

If you are saved but not baptized in the Holy Spirit with the evidence of speaking in tongues, I absolutely recommend this. This is a part of your inheritance in Christ Jesus but it must be received.

The Baptism of the Holy Spirit is for all believers and takes place when we ask our Heavenly Father, in the Name of Jesus, to baptize (or immerse) us with His Spirit. The Bible says that this Baptism is a gift from God. The only prerequisite for this gift other than being saved is to desire it. When you ask for this Baptism and truly want it, Jesus immerses you with the Holy Spirit who completely **fills** you to overflowing with Himself.

As you read this next scripture reference notice that Jesus was baptized with the Holy Spirit when the Holy Spirit descended from heaven and came upon Him. This was right after Jesus was water baptized. Since it was necessary for Jesus to be baptized with the Holy Spirit, it is equally important for you to be baptized with His Spirit.

> *"As soon as Jesus was baptized, he went up out of the water. At that moment heaven was opened, and he saw the **Spirit of God** descending like a dove and lighting on him. And a voice from heaven said, "This is my Son, whom I love; with him I am well pleased" (Matthew 3:16-17, emphasis added).*

Jesus was baptized with the Holy Spirit at the beginning of His ministry. God the Father knew that Jesus would need the Holy Spirit to complete His ministry on earth.

> *"I would not have known him, except that the one who sent me to baptize with water told me, "The man on whom you see the Spirit come down and remain is he who will baptize with the Holy Spirit" (John 1:33).*

Jesus will baptize you with His Spirit. All you need to do is ask Him.

> *"Which of you fathers, if your son asks for a fish, will give him a snake instead? Or if he asks for an egg, will give him a scorpion? If you then, though you are evil, know how to give good gifts to your children, **how much more will your Father in heaven give the Holy Spirit to those who ask him!**" (Luke 11:11–13, emphasis added)*

There is an exclamation mark at the end of this scripture. This means that there is a great emphasis put on this statement in scripture. When you ask to be baptized with the Holy Spirit, you will be given the Holy Spirit, not something else.

"When they arrived, they prayed for them that they might receive the Holy Spirit, because the Holy Spirit had not yet come upon any of them; they had simply been baptized into the name of the Lord Jesus. Then Peter and John placed their hands on them and they received the Holy Spirit" (Acts 8:15–17).

The people had already been baptized into Christ Jesus. In other words, they received Jesus into their life and were saved. Peter and John felt that it was necessary for them to be baptized with the Holy Spirit as well and, therefore, prayed for them by laying their hands on them.

*"On one occasion, while he was eating with them, he gave them this command: "Do not leave Jerusalem, but wait for **the gift** my Father promised, which you have heard me speak about. For John baptized with water, but in a few days you will be baptized with the Holy Spirit" (Acts 1:4-5, emphasis added).*

The baptism of the Holy Spirit is a gift that God wants to give to every believer. It is not just for a few but for all. However, a gift must be received.

I want to show you the importance and benefits of being baptized with the Holy Spirit.

First of all, Jesus said to wait for the gift my Father promised and He goes on to say that they would be baptized with the Holy Spirit. Jesus specifically told them to wait. Why? So that He could baptize them with His Spirit. Jesus never did anything without a purpose.

Let's look at some scriptures that show Jesus' purpose in baptizing His children with His Spirit.

*"But you will **receive power** when the Holy Spirit comes on you; and you will **be my witnesses** in Jerusalem, and in all Judea and Samaria, and to the ends of the earth" (Acts 1:8, emphasis added).*

When the 120 in the upper room were baptized with the Holy Spirit, they received **power** from the Holy Spirit (the 3rd person of) the Trinity) and they were able to go out into all the world and be **witnesses for God**. Do you remember how Peter was so afraid when Jesus was arrested and out of fear he denied knowing Jesus three times? But after he was baptized with the Holy Spirit, he boldly proclaimed the good news about Jesus. He gave his first sermon on the day he was baptized with the Holy Spirit and 3,000 people were added to the Kingdom of God that day. There was a boldness, an anointing and a power that Peter had never experienced before.

We, too, will receive power from the Holy Spirit and be bold witnesses for God as we allow His Spirit to move in and through us.

In this next scripture, notice that the people began to speak in other tongues (other languages) when they were baptized with the Holy Spirit.

*"All of them were filled with the Holy Spirit and **began to speak in other tongues as the Spirit enabled them"** (Acts 2:4, emphasis added).*

Speaking in tongues is speaking in a language that we do not know, but somewhere in the world there are people who actually speak that language. We call this our prayer language. In Acts 2:11 it says that those who were speaking in tongues were declaring the wonders of God.

Now the word "filled" with the Holy Spirit in Acts 2:4 means to imbue, influence, supply and furnish. I looked up the word "imbue" in the Webster's dictionary and it says to wet, to permeate (with ideas, emotions, etc.)

I thought this was very interesting. The Holy Spirit permeates us with His ideas, with His emotions and with His thoughts. He enlightens our minds, etc. We need this in order to walk in victory.

*"In the same way, the Spirit **helps us** in our weakness. We do not know what we ought to pray, but the **Spirit himself intercedes for us** with groans that words cannot express. And he who searches our hearts*

71

knows the mind of the Spirit, because the Spirit inter-
cedes for the saints in accordance with God's Will"
(Romans 8:26-27, emphasis added).

When we don't know how to pray in our native tongue, we can pray with our heavenly tongue. Praying in tongues helps us to be sensitive to God's Spirit. We begin to hear more clearly what God is saying to us. We begin to understand how He is guiding us. We receive wisdom from above. The gifts of the Holy Spirit that I mentioned earlier in this Chapter begin to flow from us as we align our spirit with His Spirit by praying in tongues.

"He who speaks in a tongue edifies himself"
(1 Corinthians 14:4a).

This scripture says that when we speak in tongues, we are edified which means built up, strengthened, encouraged and comforted in the most holy faith.

Do you need God to build you up, to strengthen you, to encourage you and to comfort you? I know I do. When we pray in tongues, this is what happens.

"For anyone who speaks in a tongue does not speak
to men but to God" (1 Corinthians 14:2a).

We are communicating with God when we pray in tongues. Sometimes I just desire to pray in tongues. When I do this, I am communicating with God and I am being edified at the same time.

In the next scripture, notice that they not only spoke in tongues but they **prophesied** when they were baptized in the Holy Spirit.

"When Paul placed his hands on them, the Holy Spirit
came on them, and they spoke in tongues and proph-
esied" (Acts 19:6).

"Follow the way of love and eagerly desire spiritual
gifts especially the gift of prophecy. But everyone

*who prophesies speaks to men for their strengthening,
encouragement and comfort" (1 Corinthians 14:1,3).*

When I pray in the Spirit, I am edified, strengthened, built up, encouraged and comforted so that I can now go forth in the power of the Holy Spirit and prophesy over others for their encouragement, strengthening and comfort.

These are just a few of the more obvious reasons why Jesus told His disciples to wait for the gift His father had promised which was the infilling or baptism of the Holy Spirit. Therefore, I urge you to be baptized with the Holy Spirit if you aren't already. Don't delay any longer. It is an essential step in a believer's life and part of the elementary teachings set out in Hebrews 6:1-2 so that we can go on to maturity.

Prayer for the Baptism of the Holy Spirit

Father God, in the Name of Jesus, I desire to be baptized with Your Holy Spirit just as Your disciples were on the Day of Pentecost. Jesus I ask You now to completely immerse me with Your Spirit. Father God, in Jesus Name, just as Your disciples began to speak in tongues when they were filled with Your Spirit, I desire to speak in tongues. Holy Spirit I ask that You would enable me to speak in tongues and give me utterance for the glory of God. I receive this free gift from You Father. I receive my prayer language, in Jesus' Name.

You have now been baptized with the Holy Spirit. Open your mouth and begin **by faith** to speak but not in any known language. Begin to utter syllables and expect **by faith** that the Holy Spirit will give you your prayer language. He will not hold this back from you. **By faith**, open your mouth and begin to speak as you feel it bubbling up from within you. It may sound like baby talk at the beginning but just keep on going and it will begin to flow. At first you may only get a few syllables but God will add to your prayer language and give you more as you use what He gives you. If you get a whole lot right away, praise God. If you need help in releasing your prayer language, ask God to lead you to someone who will be able to help you.

7. Jesus' Anointing

Jesus' anointing is part of our inheritance. WOW! The Holy Spirit showed me this in the middle of one night.

> *"But these are written (recorded) in order that you may believe that Jesus is the Christ (the **Anointed One**), the Son of God, and that through believing and cleaving to and trusting and relying upon him you may have life through (in) His name [through Who He is]"* *(John 20:31, Amplified, emphasis added).*

You have inherited Jesus' anointing. Have you ever thought about that? Jesus Christ is the Anointed One and He lives in you with His anointing. You have His anointing on the inside of you now. Did you know that you are an anointed child of God? This is who you are in Christ Jesus. Be established in the truth that you are first and foremost God's child. You are His son/daughter. I pray that you will get a revelation of this. Say "I am Your anointed son/daughter. I am Your anointed child". Also, if you are married, you are an anointed spouse. If you have children, you are an anointed parent. If you have a job or own a business, you are anointed in your career. You are anointed in the call of God on your life. If you are an Intercessor, you are an anointed Intercessor. If you are called into the Ministry of Helps, you are anointed to help. **You need to see yourself this way. This is how God sees you.** If you don't know this, you will not draw on Jesus' anointing. **You need to draw from that anointing that is within you.** You need to recognize this as your inheritance in Christ Jesus and partake of it and declare it over your life. Say, I am an anointed, and then fill in the blanks.

8. The Gospel

In Jesus' Last Will and Testament He left to us the Gospel. Now the word "Gospel" in the Strong's exhaustive concordance means good news, a good message. **What is this good message** that Jesus left us as an inheritance. The New Testament refers to the Gospel of Jesus, the Gospel of God, the Gospel of Peace and the Gospel of Grace. We know that there is only one Gospel so when the Word refers to the Gospel of Jesus, the Gospel of God, the Gospel of Peace and the Gospel of Grace, they are the same. The Gospel of Jesus is the Gospel of God, the Gospel of Grace and the Gospel of Peace. Jesus is God. Jesus is Grace. Jesus is Peace.

Paul preached the message of grace in Acts 14:3 "So Paul & Barnabas spent considerable time there, speaking boldly for the Lord, who confirmed the **message of his grace** by enabling them to do miraculous signs and wonders." Their message was the message of grace. The Bible says that miraculous signs and wonders will follow the preaching and the teaching of the Word. When we preach and teach the message of His grace, signs and wonders will follow. When we receive the grace of God (the Gospel) as our inheritance, miraculous signs and wonders will follow us.

I will elaborate more on the grace of God in the Chapter: Receiving God's Grace and Gift Of Righteousness Brings Joy.

9. His Name and His authority

"The seventy- two returned with joy and said, "Lord even the demons submit to us in your name" (Luke 10:17, emphasis added).

"Therefore God exalted him to the highest place and gave him the name that is above every name, that at the name of Jesus every knee should bow, in heaven and on earth and under the earth, and every tongue confess that Jesus Christ is Lord, to the glory of God the Father" (Philippians 2:9-11, emphasis added).

Jesus has given us His Name and His authority to use as our inheritance. When we go to a lawyer and sign a Power of Attorney we are giving the person we appoint as our Attorney the authority to make decisions and do things as if we were doing it ourselves. When we use Jesus' Name every angel, every negative emotion and every demon must surrender to His Name. When we use His Name, it is as if Jesus was saying it Himself. Don't talk to the demons. Simply take authority over them in Jesus' Name. We can use His Name to release healing into our bodies as well as others. There are many things that we will benefit from when we use His Name. His Name is mighty to the pulling down of strongholds. His Name has the highest authority in heaven, on earth and under the earth. There is no greater Name than the Name of Jesus.

Just simply speaking out the Name of Jesus is powerful. Try it now. Just close your eyes, focus on Jesus and slowly say His Name a few times.

10. Household Salvation

It is God's Will for our children and grandchildren to a thousand generations to be saved and know the goodness of the Lord in the land of the living. **Christ redeemed us from the curse of the law by becoming a curse for us, and since He was nailed to the cross, we can say that the curse over our family was nailed to the cross. He redeemed us in order that the blessing given to Abraham might flow in our family's lives (see Galatians 3:13-14).** However, we need to receive and declare His blessings. Deuteronomy 28:4 says that the fruit of our womb is blessed. The fruit of our womb is our children. Because I believe in Jesus and because of Jesus' obedience to the cross, I can claim this scripture that the fruit of my womb is blessed. I declare often that my children and grandchildren are blessed to a thousand generations.

> *"Know therefore that the Lord your God is God; he is the faithful God, keeping his covenant of love to **a thousand generations** of those who love him and keep his commands" (Deuteronomy 7:9, emphasis added).*

If you believe in Jesus, God has made a covenant of love with you and with your descendants to **a thousand generations**. This is awesome! You don't have to do everything perfect before God in order to receive this promise. The criteria for this promise is to believe it and receive it. God is not a God that He should lie. What He promises us in His Word, we can believe and stand on firmly. He is faithful and He will do it (see 1 Thessalonians 5:24, *emphasis added*).

> *"Can plunder be taken from warriors, or captives rescued from the fierce? But this is what the Lord says: Yes, captives will be taken from warriors, and plunder retrieved from the fierce; I will contend with those who contend with you, **and your children I will save**" (Isaiah 49:24-25, emphasis added).*

God promises us household salvation. God was speaking to Israel in this scripture. However, if you are a believer in Jesus, you are part of spiritual Israel and God is saying the same thing to you today. He says in this scripture that He will save your children. He will retrieve your children that have been taken captive. He will contend or fight for your children. In fact, Jesus has already fought and won the battle for your children. He did it all on the cross for you. Your fight is the good fight of faith. Take back what the enemy has stolen. Take back your children. How do you do this? By believing in God's promises and He will bring it to pass. Why? Because He is faithful.

> *"The Redeemer will come to Zion, to those in Jacob who repent of their sins, declares the Lord. As for me, this is my **covenant** with them, says the Lord. My Spirit, who is on you and my words that I have put in your mouth will not depart from your mouth, **or from the mouths of your children, or from the mouths of their descendants from this time on and forever**, says the Lord" (Isaiah 59:20-21, emphasis added).*

This scripture says that Jesus, our Redeemer, is with all who have repented of their sins and turned to Him. If you have received Jesus as your Savior and confess Him as your Lord, your sins are forgiven. You are in a covenant with Jesus and His covenant is with you and with your children from this time on and forever.

The covenant is that the Lord will bless us and our descendants. The curse over us and our children has been nailed to the cross and the blessings of God are released and flowing. How can the blessings flow, if we still think we are under a curse. I say "Thank you Father that the curse over me and my family has been nailed to the cross and the blessings of God are released and flowing in our lives and in our relationships, in Jesus' Name." I declare this over myself, my family and my loved ones regularly.

> *"But as for me **and my household**, we will serve the Lord" (Joshua 24:15d, emphasis added).*

Joshua understood covenant. He understood that he and his household were in a covenant with God and therefore he could say "As for me and my household, we will serve the Lord". Joshua had committed himself to believe in the God of Abraham, Isaac and Jacob. He had no foreign god before Him. If we believe in Jesus and in Jesus alone, we are in a covenant with Him and we too can say "As for me and my household, we will serve the Lord". We are declaring this **by faith** because we know that God is faithful to keep His covenant with us and with our descendants to a thousand generations.

> *"When it snows, she has no fear for her **household**; for all of them are clothed in **scarlet**. She watches over the affairs of her **household** and does not eat the bread of idleness" (Proverbs 31:21,27, emphasis added).*

This woman is referred to today as the Proverbs 31 woman. It says in verse 30 that she is a woman who fears the Lord. I believe this is the key verse. This means that she is a woman who honors the Lord and reveres Him. She allows God to order her steps and her steps lead her to watch over the affairs of her household. She makes sure that her household is clothed in scarlet. Scarlet is a very bright red color. What does this mean? Scarlet is symbolic of Jesus' shed blood for you in whom you have redemption, the forgiveness of sins. She was symbolically covering her household with the shed blood of Jesus so that when the snow or elements or negative circumstances came near them, they were well protected. Today, you can be like this Proverbs 31 woman, even if you are a man, and you can cover your household with the precious blood of Jesus which **protects them** from the not so nice elements of this world.

> *"He then brought them out and asked, "Sirs, what must I do to be saved?" They replied, "Believe in the Lord Jesus, and you will be saved – you and your household. (Acts 16:30-31, emphasis added).*

This was when Paul & Silas were in prison. They were praying and singing to God and suddenly there was an earthquake that shook the foundations of the prison and the doors of the cells flew open and all the prisoner's chains came loose. When the jailer saw this he thought that all the prisoners had escaped and so he drew his sword to kill himself but Paul stopped him by shouting that they were all there. That's when he said to Paul & Silas "What must I do to be saved" and they responded "Believe in the Lord Jesus, and you will be saved – **you and your household**". The jailer then brought Paul and Silas into his house and they spoke the Word of the Lord to the jailer and his house and he and his whole family got saved. The jailer was **filled with joy** because he had come to believe in God – he and his whole family (see Acts 16:34).

God is concerned for your whole family. Because you believe in Jesus, He will make sure that your family is saved. Your part is to believe that He will do it. Keep looking at Jesus and not at how your family is acting. Keep your eyes on Jesus, keep His promises in your heart and coming out of your mouth and you will see His promise of household salvation come to your family.

> *"The following day he arrived in Caesarea. Cornelius was expecting them and had called together his relatives and close friends" (Acts 10:24, emphasis added).*

Cornelius was a devout and God-fearing man but he was not saved yet. God gave him a vision where he saw an angel who told him to send for Peter who was staying in Joppa. Because he was **expecting** Peter to come, he brought to his house all his relatives and close friends. When Peter arrived, he told them the good news of Jesus Christ and they believed and were saved – him and his whole household including his friends. I think the key message in this whole passage of scripture was that Cornelius was **expecting** Peter to arrive. He was **expecting** to receive something from Peter for himself, his relatives and friends because of the angel's words to him. You can **expect** great things for yourself, your household and your friends because of God's promises to you. I would encourage you to have a heart of expectation as you pray for your household. Thank God for His promise of household salvation and declare His Word over your household and expect Him to move.

I would like to add here that your household is not automatically saved. They still need to make a personal decision for Christ because they have a free will but we can stand on God's promises in His Word to believe that they will freely make this personal commitment. This is the reason why I am giving you scriptures on household salvation so that you will be able to stand on God's promises and believe for your household. When we pray and declare God's Word, He is faithful to watch over His Word to bring it to pass.

Let's look at Noah. God saved his whole family from the flood including his daughters-in-law.

> *"The Lord then said to Noah, "Go into the ark, you and your whole family, because I have found you righteous" (Genesis 7:1).*

It was because Noah was found righteous by God that God saved his family from the flood. God considered Noah righteous because Noah believed God and since he believed God, he did what God told him to do and that was to build an ark. If Noah would not have built the ark, he and his family would not have been saved from the flood waters.

God considers you righteous when you believe in Jesus and because you believe, God will save your household just like He did for Noah. As I said, Noah's family included his daughters-in-law as well.

> *"**By faith** Noah, when warned about things not yet seen, in holy fear built an ark **to save his family**" (Hebrews 11:7a, emphasis added).*

Noah had never seen rain. God watered the garden in Eden from streams that came up from the earth (see Genesis 2:5-6) not from rain. There is no mention in scripture of it having rained until the flood. So when it says in the above scripture that Noah was warned about things not yet seen, it is referring to Noah having never seen it rain before the flood waters came. **By faith**, Noah in holy fear built an ark to save his family.

Just like Noah, we have to believe God's promises for household salvation and do what He tells us to do. We have to believe that household salvation has already been provided for in the finished work of Christ and then receive it. It is **by faith** in His finished work and His promises that the manifestation of salvation to our household will come. Household salvation is part of our inheritance in Christ Jesus. We must first of all believe that God promises us household salvation and then we need to receive it. An inheritance will never be ours if we do not know that it belongs to us and if we do not receive it.

> *"The Lord said to Moses and Aaron in Egypt. This month is to be for you the first month, the first month of your year. Tell the whole community of Israel that on the tenth day of this month each man is to take a lamb for his family, one for each household" (Exodus 12:1-3).*

We know that the lamb referred to in this scripture is a shadow or type of Jesus.

> *"Then they are to take some of the blood and put it on the sides and tops of the doorframes of **the houses** where they eat the lambs. On that same night I will pass through Egypt and strike down every firstborn – both men and animals – and I will bring judgment on all the gods of Egypt. I am the Lord. The blood will be*

*a sign for you on **the houses** where you are; and when
I see the blood, I will pass over you. No destructive
plaque will touch you when I strike Egypt" (Exodus
12:7, 12-13, emphasis added).*

The Israelites were instructed by God to kill a lamb and put its blood on the sides and tops of the doorframes of their houses. Everyone in that house were saved from the angel of death because of the blood of the lamb that was on those houses. I regularly cover myself, my family and my loved ones with the precious blood of Jesus for protection from the enemy. Although I have not mentioned it separately in this Book, the blood of Jesus is also part of our inheritance.

*"Then tell them, "It is the Passover sacrifice to the
Lord, who passed over **the houses** of the Israelites in
Egypt and spared **our homes** when he struck down the
Egyptians" (Exodus 12:27, emphasis added).*

God spared whole households because they believed God and did what He told them to do. Whatever God tells you to pray for your family, do it. Whatever promises you find in His Word to declare over your family, do it.

We have briefly mentioned Rahab before but I would like to elaborate on the scriptures concerning Rahab a little more.

*"Now then, please swear to me by the Lord that you
will show kindness **to my family**, because I have
shown kindness to you. Give me a sure sign that
you will spare the lives of my father and mother, my
brothers and sisters, and all who belong to them, and
that you will **save us** from death" (Joshua 2:12-13,
emphasis added).*

Rahab did not have any children but she was believing for the salvation of her whole family which consisted of her father, mother, brothers and sisters and all their families.

Let's look at what happened in Joshua 6:22, 23, 25 "Joshua said to the two men who had spied out the land, Go into the prostitute's house and bring her out and all who belong to her, in accordance with your oath to her. So the young men who had done the spying went in and brought out Rahab, her father and mother and brothers and all who belonged to her. They brought out her entire family and put them in a place outside the camp of Israel. But Joshua spared **Rahab the prostitute, with her family and all who belonged to her**, because she hid the men Joshua had sent as spies to Jericho – and she lives among the Israelites to this day."

Rahab believed in the God of the Israelites and because of her belief and because she put the scarlet cord outside her window and because she brought all her family into her house, as she was instructed by the two spies, they were saved. The things she did were not burdensome to her. They were simple instructions that she followed and she did them because she believed that her and her whole family would be saved.

Are you believing God for your whole family to be saved? Can you see that God promises us household salvation? His Word is very clear. Our part is to believe that He will do it.

In 2 Chronicles Chapter 20 there were three armies coming to make war against Jehoshaphat, the King of Judah. They were much larger and stronger than the people of Judah. Jehoshaphat prayed and at the end of his prayer he said "We don't know what to do but our eyes are upon you". Isn't that how we feel when we are faced with an impossible situation. The thief is trying to come against our families to keep them from believing and living for God. God responded to Jehoshaphat's prayer and said "Do not be afraid or discouraged because of this vast army. For the battle is not yours, but God's". God is saying the same thing to us today. Do not be afraid or discouraged because of the enemy for the battle is not ours, but God's. Then Jehoshaphat encourages the people and says "Have faith in the Lord your God and you will be upheld". As the people began to sing and praise God, **the Lord set ambushes** against these vast armies who were coming against them and they defeated each other. Judah did not have to fight these armies. God did it. God set the ambushes. Jehoshaphat and his men went in and carried off the plunder which was more than they could take away. This Chapter shows us that even though the enemy is fierce who is trying to come against our households, when we put our faith in God and worship Him, He will do what only He can do and we will go in and carry away our whole households.

> *"He took with him to Egypt his sons and grandsons and his daughters and granddaughters – all his offspring" (Genesis 46:7).*

This scripture is talking about Jacob and his whole household. God saved Jacob and his whole household from starvation and death. He brought them to Egypt and Pharaoh gave them the best land in Egypt to live in.

> *"Crispus, the synagogue ruler and **his entire household** believed in the Lord" (Acts 18:8a, emphasis added).*

Don't be weighed down with trying to save your children. God has already made provision for you and your household through the finished works of Jesus. Believe God and receive household salvation. Thank Him for it regularly.

At the end of this Chapter, I have included a prayer that you can pray over your family.

In this Chapter, I have told you about a number of things that are part of our inheritance.

Paul told Timothy in 1 Timothy 1:6 to fan into flame the gift of God. Your inheritance is a gift to you from Jesus Christ Himself. Now it is up to you to fan into flame these gifts, **with the help of the Holy Spirit**, so that they will become a reality in your life. It is not by your might or by your power but by His Spirit that you can fan into flame these gifts. Ask the Holy Spirit to help you.

Jesus has deposited all these things into your heavenly bank account which actually is inside of you. Now it is up to you to make withdrawals by fertilizing and watering what is on the inside of you. You shouldn't let your inheritance just sit stagnate in your bank account. You need to know what your inheritance is so that you can receive it and benefit from it.

There are many more truths to be discovered and unfolded to us in His word that is part of our inheritance in Christ Jesus. I pray that the Holy Spirit would reveal to us what is our inheritance in Christ Jesus more and more in these last days.

Prayer for your family

Thank you Father that Jesus came to preach good news to my family, to bind up the brokenhearted in my family, to proclaim freedom for my family and release from darkness for my family, to proclaim the year of the Lord's favor and the day of vengeance of my God, to comfort all who mourn and provide for those who grieve in Zion, to bestow on them a crown of beauty instead of ashes, the oil of gladness instead of mourning and a garment of praise instead of a spirit of despair. Therefore, I declare that my family is receiving the good news of the Gospel of Grace that Jesus brought. I declare God's favor in my relationship with my family and every area of life. I declare that my family is freed from all darkness and demonic activity. I declare satan's defeat over my family. I declare that my family is saved, comforted, healed and made whole in every area of life. I declare that my family is walking in the victory that Jesus accomplished for us in His redemptive work.

Thank you Father for Your promises of household salvation. When I read Your Word I see that Noah and his family were saved, that Rahab and her family were saved, that Cornelius and his family were saved. I see Your promises of household salvation throughout Your Word. Therefore, I declare by faith that my household is saved (spirit, soul and body). Father, help me to believe this and to receive my inheritance of household salvation expecting you for the manifestation to come forth quickly, in Jesus' Name.

Help me and my family to conduct ourselves in a manner worthy of the Gospel of Christ.

May the grace and peace of the Lord Jesus Christ be upon me and my family.

I cover myself and my family with the precious blood of Jesus.

Thank You Father that me and my family will not run ahead of You and birth Ishmaels but that we will wait upon You and allow You to birth Isaacs through us, in Jesus' Name.

Thank You Father, in Jesus' Name, that my children are commending Your works to their children (my grandchildren), they are telling of Your mighty acts to their children. They are speaking of the glorious splendor of Your majesty to their children. They are meditating on Your wonderful works. They are telling of the power of Your awesome works to their children. They are proclaiming Your great deeds to their children. They are celebrating Your abundant goodness and joyfully singing of Your righteousness with their children.

May the God of peace sanctify me and my family through and through and may our whole spirit, soul and body be kept blameless at the coming of our Lord Jesus Christ.

Father thank You for binding me and my family together in love and for bringing me and my family into complete unity in the Holy Spirit and in the faith, in Jesus' Name.

Thank You Father that Jesus became a curse for us and He was nailed to the cross. Therefore I declare that the curse is destroyed over me and my family and the blessings of God are flowing. Thank You Father that the fruit of my womb is blessed. When the enemy comes at me and my family in one direction he is defeated before us and must flee in seven directions. Thank You for an open heaven over my family. Thank You that me and my family are blessed coming in and going out, that the blessings of God are chasing after and overtaking my family, in Jesus' Name.

Thank You Father that Jesus Christ, the anointed One, lives in me and therefore, I am anointed because of Christ's anointing that resides in me. I declare that my children are anointed to parent their children. I declare that my sons are anointed to take their rightful place as the heads of their homes, they are anointed to father their children and to bring them up in the training and instruction of the Lord. I declare that my children and their perspective spouses, out of reverence for Christ, are loving and respecting each other and submitting to each other. I declare that my children and grandchildren, out of reverence for Christ, are obeying and honoring their parents.

Thank You Father that no weapon formed against me and my family will prosper. God You are for us, nothing can be against them. Thank You Father for binding us together with cords of love that cannot be broken. Thank You Father that Your plans for us are good and that You give us hope and a future, in Jesus' Name.

Thank You Father for preparing the hearts of every family member so that when they hear the Word of God, the seeds will be planted into rich fertile soil and will spring forth producing a crop of one thousand fold, in Jesus' Name.

Thank You Father that my family is believing right in accordance with Your Word and walking in and fulfilling the call of God on each one of their lives, that they are anchored in Your love, walking in intimacy with You, Jesus and Holy Spirit and are receiving Your abundant provision of grace and gift of righteousness to reign in life through Jesus Christ, in Jesus' Name.

Thank You Father for sending forth Your anointed laborers to my family, speaking Your anointed Word to them and breaking and destroying the yokes of bondage and setting my family free by the Truth, in Jesus' Name.

I thank You that no harm will befall me and my family, no disaster will come near us for You command Your angels concerning us to guard us in all our ways, they lift us up in their hands so that not one in my family will strike their foot against a stone, in Jesus' Name.

Thank You Father for helping me and my family to grasp how wide and long and high and deep is the love of Christ for us personally and to know Your love by experience so that we may be filled to overflowing with Your love. Thank You Father that You are doing immeasurably, exceedingly, abundantly above and beyond all that we could ever ask imagine or think according to Your great power within us. Thank You for filling us with the knowledge of Your will through all spiritual wisdom and understanding and Your grace to walk wholeheartedly in Your will for our lives, in Jesus' Name.

Thank You Father that my family is seeking first Your kingdom and Your righteousness and that everything else is falling into place in their lives, in Jesus' Name.

Thank You Father for giving us the spirit of wisdom and revelation so that we may know You better, that out of Your glorious riches of grace You are strengthening us in our inner being by Your Spirit so that Christ dwells in our hearts through faith, in Jesus' Name.

Now Father I commit my family into Your hands, I declare Your Lordship over my family and I stand together with You as one in the Spirit believing You for the miraculous, the supernatural and the extraordinary regarding my life and the lives of my family, in Jesus' Name.

Receiving God's Grace And His Gift Of Righteousness Brings Joy

*W*hat is grace? It is undeserved, unearned, unmerited favor of God to us. Grace cannot be earned, deserved or merited. It can only be received.

> *"For, if by the trespass of the one man, death reigned through that one man, how much more will those who receive God's **abundant provision of grace and of the gift of righteousness reign in life through the one man, Jesus Christ**"* *(Romans 5:17, emphasis added).*

God's grace and His gift of righteousness is part of our inheritance in Christ Jesus. The promise of God in the above scripture says we will **reign in life** if we receive His abundant provision of grace and His gift of righteousness. I declare this scripture often over my life. I need God's grace and gift of righteousness in my life to reign over every situation and circumstance I find myself in. When I think of reigning, I think of royalty. We will reign like kings and priests of the Most High God. The Bible says in 1 Peter 2:9 that we are a chosen people, a royal priesthood, a holy nation, a people belonging to God. I do not rely on myself to reign in life but I rely on God's grace and His gift of righteousness to reign in life through Jesus Christ.

When I first began to understand and receive God's grace and to walk in it day by day, this truth set me free from a **roller coaster ride**.

I would be up and down. God wants us on **level ground (stable).** I experienced **deep dark times of total despair** when I did not even want to live but God set me free as I embraced the message of His grace and received His gift of righteousness.

Abraham, Isaac and Jacob all lived under grace as the law had not yet been given.

Abraham was a man who believed God and simply did what God told him to do. There was no law for him to follow. It was a simple relationship between God and Abraham. Abraham believed God and, therefore, he did what God told him to do. Because Abraham believed in God, he was right with God. God credited Abraham's belief in Him with righteousness (see James 2:23). Although he was right with God, Abraham did not do everything right. He lied to a King and told him that Sarah was his sister so that the King would not kill him. He did some other things as well that would not be considered righteous acts. Even though some of Abraham's actions were wrong, he himself was right with God because he believed in God.

What about you? Do you believe that you are right with God even when you have just done some wrong things? Do you believe that all your sins are forgiven (past, present & future sins)? Your answers to these questions are very important as they determine what you believe.

When a little boy is told that he is bad because of something he has done and if he is told it often enough, he believes that he is bad and bad actions will follow. However, if he is told that he had done a bad thing but that he is still a good boy and Mommy and Daddy still love him even though he had done a bad thing, that little boy will grow up believing that he is right and his actions will follow what he believes about himself. Because he believes that he is right, he will do right.

When we believe that our sins are forgiven, that we are saved by grace, that we are the righteousness of God in Christ Jesus and that there is now no condemnation for those who are in Christ Jesus, we will reign over sorrow and grief. We will reign over temptations. We will reign over sickness and disease, etc. through Christ Jesus and we will do right. **When we believe right, our actions will follow. When we believe right, our emotions will be healed and we will be made whole.**

Are you currently struggling with sin in your life? The Bible says that sin shall not reign or have power in your life when you **believe** that you are under grace and no longer under the law. Let's look at that scripture. Pay very close attention to the rest of this Chapter so that you receive the revelation that the Holy Spirit desires to give you.

> *"For sin shall **not** be your master because you are **not under law but under grace"** (Romans 6:14, emphasis added).*

What a powerful scripture. When you live under grace, sin has no more power over you. That's what this scripture says. Please read it again. If you are struggling with sin, it is because you are still trying to overcome that sin in your own power instead of relying on and believing God to set you free by His grace. When you rely on your own power to be set free from sin, you are still living under the law and not under grace. When you rely on God's grace alone to set you free and believe that He will do it, that sin will lose its power over you and you will be free.

As a believer, you are the righteousness of God in Christ Jesus? Let's look at the scripture that says that.

> *"But now **a righteousness** from God, **apart from the law**, has been made known, to which the law and the prophets testify. This righteousness from God comes **through faith in Jesus Christ to all who believe"** (Romans 3:21-22, emphasis added).*

Did you see that righteousness comes not from the law but by faith in Jesus Christ? Wow! This is good news. This is the Gospel of Jesus Christ. This is the Gospel of His grace. This is truth that will set you free from the power of sin.

Jesus is for us and not against us. Jesus' death and resurrection made the difference for us who believe. Jesus is the end of the law (see Romans 10:4).

Unbelievers who live under the law have a **sin consciousness** which keeps them in bondage to sin (cycle of sin) until they come to

Christ Jesus. The law is good and does what it was put in place to do. It condemns people and helps them to realize they are sinners in need of a Savior, but it cannot save them. The law cannot save people. It can only condemn people of their sin which actually causes people under the law to sin even more. However, once we come to Christ, we don't need the law anymore as it did what it was supposed to do. It brought us to Jesus. We are now saved by grace through faith in Christ Jesus. We live our Christian life the same way we got saved (by grace through faith in Christ Jesus). We, as believers, are not to go back under the law because by doing so we are saying Jesus has not made a difference in our life. We are saying His work on the cross for us was not complete. If we believe Jesus has made us righteous, we will have a **righteousness consciousness** and this, along with the grace of God, will cause us to reign over sin. Knowing we are sinners does not set us free from sin, but knowing that we have been made righteous by the blood of the lamb and that all our sins are forgiven will break the power of sin in our lives and set us free from it. The law of the Spirit of life sets us free from the law of sin and death (see Romans 8:2). Jesus came to give us life and to give it to us more abundantly (see John 10:10b).

I hear believers say that they are sinners saved by grace. This is not correct. If we are saved, then we are no longer a sinner. This is no longer our identity. Our identity as a believer is that we are the righteousness of God in Christ Jesus. We are now saints who sometimes sin but we are no longer identified as a sinner. We are a new creation in Christ Jesus. The old has gone and the new has come. We were a sinner (past tense) but we are now the righteousness of God in Christ Jesus (present tense). What is it that a sinner does? A sinner goes out and sins. As a believer, I do not want to be identified as a sinner because this identity will cause me to sin. However, if I identify myself as the righteousness of God in Christ Jesus, it will cause me to live right.

Under the Old Covenant, once a year the priests would offer up sacrifices to God on behalf of the people and the High Priest would take the blood into the Holy of Holies and sprinkle it on the mercy seat to cover the sins of the people that had been committed over the previous year. This was done every year because of the new sins the people committed. Each year it was to cover only the sins that had been committed over the past year, not any future sins. However, Jesus was offered up, once for all, for all our sins (past, present and future sins). So when we come to Jesus, all of our sins are cleansed and forgiven. We are made right with God once for all time **as long as we believe in Him**.

Again, under the Old Covenant, man would offer a Sin Offering to God by bringing an innocent perfect spotless lamb to the priest. The priest would examine the lamb, **not the man**, to make sure it was perfect and without defect. The man then laid his hands on the lamb and the man's sins were imputed or transferred to the lamb. The Sin Offering speaks of Jesus (our perfect, sinless Lamb) taking our sins on His own body on the tree.

Under the Old Covenant, man would offer a Burnt Offering to God. The innocent perfect spotless lamb would be burnt up on the altar thus it would give its life for the man and impute or transfer its righteousness to the man. The lamb took the place of the man. The man should have died for his sins but the lamb died in the place of the man. The burnt offering speaks of Jesus dying for us in our place and the righteousness of Jesus being transferred to us at the cross.

The moment we believe in Jesus and invite Him into our lives as our Savior and Lord this is what takes place. He freely takes away all of our sins and freely gives us His righteousness. This is called the Divine exchange.

Because Jesus gave us His righteousness as a gift, we are now as righteous as Jesus is. We are in Him and He is in us. There is no sin in Jesus. Now, when God looks at us, He sees Jesus (the perfect, spotless, sinless lamb). He sees Jesus' righteousness in us. He no longer sees our sin because in Jesus all of our sins have been forgiven and taken away. Under the old covenant, the blood of the lamb only **covered** the sins of the people and only for one year at a time. However, Jesus' shed blood **takes away** our sins for all time. WOW!

> *"And when you were dead in your transgressions and in the uncircumcision of your flesh, He made you alive together with Him, having forgiven us **all** our transgressions, having **canceled out the certificate***

of debt consisting of decrees against us and which was hostile to us; and He has taken it out of the way, **having nailed it to the cross**. *When He had* **disarmed** *the rulers and authorities, He made a public display of them, having triumphed over them through Him"* *(Colossians 2:13-15, emphasis added).*

When we come to Jesus and believe, He forgives us of all our sins (past, present and future sins). When the scripture says "all", it means "all". Because all of our sins are now forgiven, the law (the certificate of debt in the above scripture) is no longer needed in the life of a **believer** so Jesus cancelled it for us and nailed it to the cross so that it could no longer oppose us or be hostile towards us. That's what this scripture says. By cancelling the law's power over us, He disarmed and triumphed over satan and his demons for us. Did you see that in this scripture? This means that satan and his demons can no longer use the law to condemn us and make us feel guilty and ashamed when we miss the mark. The power that satan uses to condemn us for our shortcomings is the law but, by believing in Jesus, the law and satan's accusations have no more power over us. Satan has been disarmed. The law was his ammunition. Jesus fulfilled the law perfectly for us and, as believers in Christ Jesus, God the Father sees Jesus' finished work when He looks at us. God the Father sees us as fulfilling the law through His Son, Jesus, and the law no longer is required in our lives. God has now written His law on our hearts and the New Covenant law is to believe and to love (see 1 John 3:23). We are under a new covenant now. We are under the new covenant of grace.

God is offering grace to you today, as a believer. You can choose whether you will receive His grace and live under it or you can choose to live under the law.

I said earlier that grace means undeserved, unearned and unmerited favor of God. We don't have to try to earn God's favor. In fact, God does not want us to try to earn His favor because when we do this we are actually mixing grace with the law. The law is all about our self-efforts and what we can do to earn favor with God. Grace is all about Jesus and what He has already done for us. When we embrace the grace of God, our focus changes from ourselves to Jesus. Jesus becomes our focus.

> *"Before **this faith came**, we were held **prisoners by the law, locked up until faith** should be revealed. So the law was put in charge to lead us to Christ that we might be justified by faith. **Now that faith has come, we are no longer under the supervision of the law"** (Galatians 3:23, emphasis added).*

Did you see that? Now that faith has come (now that we believe in Jesus), we are no longer under the law but under grace. Before we believed, we were held prisoners by the law, locked up until we made a choice to believe. The law, which is good, was put in place to lead us to Christ, but now that we are in Christ the law no longer has a purpose in our life. We are now under grace. Jesus has set us free from the law which is a ministry of condemnation and death and He has brought us into the ministry of His Spirit which is a ministry of life. Hallelujah!

> *"You foolish Galatians! Who has bewitched you? Before your very eyes Jesus Christ was already portrayed as crucified. I would like to learn just one thing from you: **Did you receive the Spirit by observing the law, or by believing what you heard?** Are you so foolish? **After beginning with the Spirit, are you now trying to attain your goal by human effort?** Have you suffered so much for nothing – if it really was for nothing? Does God give you His Spirit and work miracles among you **because you observe the law, or because you believe what you heard?"** (Galatians 3:1-5, emphasis added)*

Paul was talking to the Galatian believers in this scripture reference. Paul called them "foolish" and "bewitched" because they were so quick to believe these false teachers who were telling the Galatian believers that they needed to obey the law. Paul was reminding the

Galatians that they got saved by believing in Jesus, not by observing the law. He was trying to make them realize that they had gone back under the law to live their Christian life by their own human or self-efforts rather than depending on and relying on the Spirit. When we try to obey the law (which we cannot fully do), we are depending upon our self-righteousness to be acceptable and pleasing to God. What God wants is for us to receive His grace and His righteousness for there is no other righteousness that is acceptable to Him.

> *"Now it is evident that no person is justified – declared righteous and brought into right standing with God – **through the Law** for the Scripture says, The man in right standing with God (the just, the righteous) shall live by and out of faith, and he who **through and by faith** is declared righteous and in right standing with God shall live" (Galatians 3:11, Amplified, emphasis added).*

The scriptures I am referring to are very clear that we will not be made righteous by obeying the law. We are made righteous through faith in Jesus Christ alone.

> *"But the Law does not rest on faith – does not require faith, has nothing to do with faith – for it itself says, He who does them (the things prescribed by the Law) **shall live by them, [not by faith]**" (Galatians 3:12, Amplified, emphasis added).*

I had been taught that the opposite of faith is fear but this is not correct according to this scripture. The opposite of faith is not fear. The opposite of faith is the law. That's what this scripture says. The law is contrary to faith. The law has nothing to do with faith. The law is opposite to faith. The law opposes faith. God does not want us to walk by faith and walk by the law. God does not want us to mix the two together (grace and law). It doesn't work. The law is all about man's self-efforts to fulfill the law. Sometimes we try to qualify ourselves for God's blessings. This is the law, not faith. When we do this, we are actually going back under the law and trying to obtain God's blessings through our self-efforts instead of simply believing in Jesus and in His finished work on the cross of Calvary. We will never be able to receive God's blessings through our own self-efforts. God's blessings are free and must be received by grace through faith in Jesus Christ.

> *I know your deeds, that you are neither cold nor hot. I wish you were either one or the other! So, because you are lukewarm – neither hot nor cold – I am about to spit you out of my mouth"* (Revelations 3:15-16).

When Jesus said "I know your deeds" He was saying that He knew what they **believed**. He knew what was in their heart. He said that **their believing** was neither cold nor hot. He was referring to their believing not their works. He said "I wish that you were either one or the other!" He used an exclamation mark to emphasize the passion in His heart when He said this. I want to show you in scripture that Jesus was talking about their believing and not their deeds (works). When the apostles asked Jesus what they must do to do the **works** God required, **Jesus said that the works of God is to believe in Jesus** (see John 6:26-29). Please look up this scripture and see it for yourself.

Jesus was saying that **their believing** was lukewarm. What makes a Christian's believing lukewarm? A lukewarm Christian is one who believes in Jesus as their Savior and Lord and receives salvation by grace through faith in Him but then goes back to live their Christian life under the law. They mix grace and law together. They are trying to obey the law, and earn the salvation of their soul by their righteous acts, yet they think they are living under grace.

The Church has misinterpreted "lukewarmness". I have heard it preached, and I have taught it myself before I understood grace, that if you did not read your Bible enough, fast, pray and do all kinds of righteous acts that you were lukewarm. Let's be honest with ourselves. Believers rate other believers by what they do. We ask believers "What are you doing for Jesus?" We erroneously believe that a Christian who is doing all the right things outwardly and attending all the Church meetings is on fire for God. We erroneously believe that those who are

97

struggling inwardly to read their Bible and who are struggling to walk in victory over sin are lukewarm and need to rededicate their lives to God and confess their sins. We've been trying to do the work of Holy Spirit to get people to do good works and live right when, in fact, God has called us to preach the Gospel. We are to preach and teach the Gospel of Grace which lifts up the person of Jesus Christ and allow the Holy Spirit to transform people's lives. Let the Holy Spirit move. He will be able to accomplish what we can't.

Jesus looks not at your outward actions but He looks at your heart to see whether you believe in Him and in His finished work on the cross. Don't get me wrong. I am not promoting complacency in your life. I believe that when you truly embrace grace alone (not mixing it with the law), the Holy Spirit will guide you into the fullness of what God has for you. This will take time. It doesn't happen overnight. Your actions will eventually follow your right believing. **Grace creates a resolve to do good**, not permission to do bad. However, when a Christian mixes law and grace together both the law and grace lose their power. This is why Jesus said "I wish you were either hot or cold". In other words, Jesus wants people to be either completely under grace or completely under the law. If one is completely under the law, then the law is able to do its work and convict that person that they are a sinner and in need of a Savior. But if that person is mixing grace and law together, they are deceived in thinking that they are living under grace alone. They don't really understand grace.

In Jesus' redemptive work on the Cross, He fully obeyed the law for us, as believers, because He knew that we could not do it ourselves. He made us righteous by His blood, **by His grace alone**. He paid a huge price to free us from the law. He made us holy and extends His grace to us. **Grace teaches us to live upright and godly lives (see Titus 2:11-14).** Grace helps us in our times of need (see Hebrews 4:16). Our hearts are strengthened by grace (see Hebrews 13:9). When we, as believers, mix grace and law together we are saying that grace alone isn't enough and what Jesus did on the cross for us isn't enough. We are saying that Jesus' righteousness isn't enough and that we still have to make ourselves righteous by obeying the law or by earning our righteousness through our good deeds.

When we hear the law preached or taught, it instills fear into the hearts of the people. This is good if the hearers are unbelievers because they need to know that they are sinners in need of a Savior. However, when the law is taught to a believer, it causes the believer to think that the righteousness of Jesus that they received at salvation isn't enough to carry them forward in their Christian walk. It causes the believer to think that they need **to earn** the salvation of their soul when, in fact, it is a matter of renewing their minds with the Word of God and allowing the Holy Spirit freedom in their lives to make the necessary changes. Fear based messages to people who already believe in Jesus cause people to make behavior changes in their own power that can only last for a short time. Grace based messages will cause people to believe right and their hearts and **lives will be transformed by the Word of God. A lasting transformation will take place by believing right.** As people experience for themselves the love of God and the grace of God and know that they are made righteous, this will empower them to reign over sorrow, grief, sin, etc. in their lives.

Can you see how freeing this is? This is the truth that sets people free. This is the good news of Jesus Christ. This is the Gospel of Jesus Christ, the Gospel of Grace.

The following scripture is a picture of when a believer mixes grace and law together.

> *"No one sews a patch of unshrunk cloth on an old garment, for the patch will pull away from the garment, making the tear worse. Neither do people pour **new wine** into **old wineskins**. If they do, the skins will burst; the wine will run out and the **wineskins will be ruined**. No, they pour **new wine into new wineskins, and both are preserved"** (Matthew 9:16-17, emphasis added).*

Jesus was giving an illustration of what happens when believers mix grace and law together. **Grace is like the new wine** and the **Old Covenant law is like the old wineskins.** Grace is the new wine. Jesus is the new wine. Old wineskins cannot expand because they have already been used and expanded as much as they are going to expand. The old wineskin, the law, has already done its work in the life of a believer and is no longer useful for a believer. When new wine, which causes the wineskins to expand, is poured into old wine-skins, the wineskins will burst (because there is no more room for expansion) ruining the wineskins and causing the wine to be poured out making the new wine ineffective. When this happens, both the wine and wineskins are of no effect anymore. They have both lost their effectiveness and their power. He is saying that neither grace nor the law is effective when we walk in mixture. However, when new wine (Jesus, the Grace of God) is poured into new wineskins (representing the New Covenant of Grace), both are preserved and both are powerful. So you see here **grace upon grace**. You see pure unadulterated grace when new wine is poured into new wineskins. In this situation, there is no mixture and this will cause believers to be fruitful and very effective and powerful for the Kingdom of God. Jesus was saying that in order to receive the grace of God and have it be effective and powerful in your life, you have to get rid of the old wineskin (the law).

In the same way, grace is like the patch of unshrunk cloth and the Old Covenant law is like the old garment that has already been washed and shrunk. When the old garment is washed again, the new unshrunk patch will shrink and pull away from the old ruining the garment.

This is so important for you to understand. As a believer, you can unknowingly be mixing law and grace together. I did before I came to understand grace. This is the enemy's doing. He does not want you to understand that you are the righteousness of God in Christ Jesus, that you are fully accepted by Jesus and loved by God uncon-ditionally. He does not want you to understand grace in its totality because when you understand grace and walk **in grace alone** you will be very effective and flow in God's power, bearing much fruit for the Kingdom of God. The devil does not want you to be effective or fruitful in Christ Jesus. He does not want you to realize that you are now his master. He wants to keep you under the law because the law ministers death and ineffectiveness but grace ministers life and effectiveness. He is a thief and he comes to rob, steal, kill and destroy (see John 10:10a). However, Jesus came to give us abundant life, a grace filled life (see John 10:10b). The devil wants to steal from you the righteousness that Jesus died to give you by keeping you in mixture. When you feel condemned, you think you are not doing enough so you go back under the law to be made righteous instead of simply believing right which will produce right behavior and transformation. The devil wants you to think that grace is something that you will take and use as a license to sin so that you will not receive the grace of God in its totality. When you receive God's abundant provision of grace, His gift of righteousness, His unconditional love and His acceptance of you just the way you are, **you're red hot** because your believing is right. Grace will cause you to reign over sin (see Romans 5:17), not go out and sin more. In fact, if you would take this message as a license to sin, you are not believing right for sin shall not have dominion over you if you continue to believe right.

The sinner, one who has never believed in Jesus, is living under the law and is ice cold. There are only two covenants in existence today. They are the old covenant of law and the new covenant of grace. The Christian who is mixing grace and law **is lukewarm**. He is a double-minded person. The reason Jesus said He would spit the lukewarm Christian out of His mouth is because it makes Him sick to His stomach that we still think we have to add self-righteousness and add self-efforts to His finished work. He says that self-righteousness is as filthy rags to Him (see Isaiah 64:6). He paid such a huge price to save us. He suffered beyond what we could ever understand or imagine and not to receive His grace and His righteousness as a complete and total redemption causes Him to want to throw up (see Revelation 3:16).

> *"Where then is boasting? It is excluded. On what principle? On that of observing the law? No, but on that of faith" (Romans 3:27).*

People boast when they observe the law i.e. I pray this long each day. I read the Word for this long each day. I do this and I do that. It is all about them. This is boasting in the flesh. This kind of boasting does not impress God or qualify you for His blessings. What qualifies you is believing in Jesus. Our boasting should be in what Jesus has done for us and not on what we have done. Prayer is good. Bible study is good. Good works are good BUT not if we think that because of all these things we qualify ourselves for God's blessings or if we do them out of religious duty thinking that we are more righteous because of it. That is living under the law. It's all about us. However, when we do these very same things (prayer, Bible study, good works, etc.) because we believe in Jesus and we simply desire to fellowship with Him, get to know Him intimately, want our minds renewed with His Word so that we will walk in victory and want Him to flow through us and direct our actions for His glory, this, my friend, is grace. It is all about Jesus and allowing Him to bear much fruit in and through our lives. The struggle ceases and we enter into the rest of God. Resting in God is simply resting from our own good works in the flesh trying to gain God's approval. Resting in God is coming out from under the law and living under grace and receiving His grace and His gift of righteousness. **Resting in God is believing in Jesus (Jesus is our Rest)** and knowing that we are acceptable to Him just the way we are. The Israelites did not enter the rest of God because of their unbelief. They still thought they could be righteous in themselves. They still thought that they could fully obey the law in themselves. We need to come to the end of ourselves. We need to come to the end of our self-efforts and receive God's grace and gift of righteousness alone.

The rest of God is not inactivity. In fact, when you rest in God, you will bear more fruit than you would if you were not resting in Him. Entering into God's rest is believing in and receiving His finished work on the cross. Resting in God is doing whatever God leads you to do without stress and worry. It is believing in Jesus who is our Rest. When we believe right, our actions will follow our believing. We wait upon Him for specific instructions in our life until He gives us direction. In the meantime, we keep doing what the Word of God tells us to do so that our minds are renewed and our character transformed by His grace. We do it not because it makes us more righteous, not out of a sense of duty but because we now want to be more like Him in our character.

Let's continue in ROMANS 3:28-31 "For we maintain that a man is justified by faith apart from observing the law. Is God the God of

Jews only? Is he not the God of Gentiles too? Yes, of Gentiles too, since there is only one God, who will justify the circumcised by faith and the uncircumcised through that same faith. Do we, then, nullify the law by this faith? Not at all! Rather, we up hold the law."

How do we uphold the law? By faith in Jesus and in His finished work. Jesus fulfilled the law for us, as believers, and by so doing He cancelled the law and nailed it to the cross. When we believe in Jesus, God the Father sees us as having fulfilled the law. When He looks at us, He sees the finished work of Jesus. He sees us forgiven, sinless, holy and righteous. He sees the blood of Jesus, just like the destroying Angel saw the blood on the doorposts of the Israelites' homes and passed over so that the firstborn was saved.

> *"Do not think that I have come to abolish the Law or the Prophets; I have not come to abolish them but to fulfill them" (Matthew 5:17).*

Jesus did not come to abolish the law for the unbeliever because the law is needed in order to bring them to Christ. Jesus came to fulfill the law for the believer. In Ephesians 2:14-15 where Paul is talking to believers it says that Jesus destroyed the barrier, the dividing wall of hostility, by abolishing in His flesh the law with its commandments and regulations. So, those of us who are in Christ Jesus, the law has been abolished.

I want you to see from the above scripture that the law includes the ten commandments. Look up this scripture for yourself. Jesus abolished the law with its commandments and regulations.

> *"Christ **purchased our freedom (redeeming us) from the curse of the Law's (condemnation), by [Himself] becoming a curse for us**, for it is written [in the Scriptures], Cursed is everyone who hangs on a tree (is crucified). To the end that through [their receiving] Christ Jesus, the blessing [promised] to Abraham might come upon the Gentiles, so that we **through faith** might [all] receive [the realization of]*

the promise of the (Holy) Spirit" (Galatians 3:13-14, Amplified, emphasis added).

Jesus redeemed you from the curse of the law by becoming a curse for you. He destroyed the curse in your life. He destroyed the curse in my life. The curse is destroyed over your emotions, your body, your mind, your relationships, your finances, your household, etc. and the blessings of Abraham are flowing. Declare this over yourself and your loved ones. You can declare that the curse is destroyed over your emotions and that your emotions are blessed. Go ahead and do that now. Say, I declare that the curse is destroyed over my emotions and my emotions are blessed in the Name of Jesus. You can declare this over every area in your life. Please remember this and make these declarations.

"Consider Abraham: He believed God, and it was credited to him as righteousness. Understand, then, that those who believe are children of Abraham. The Scripture foresaw that God would justify the Gentiles by faith, and announced the gospel in advance to Abraham: All nations will be blessed through you.' **So those who have faith are blessed along with Abraham, the man of faith"** *(Galatians 3:6-9, emphasis added).*

Abraham became righteous by believing. This is the Gospel that was given in advance to Abraham. We become righteous and are **blessed** by simply believing in Jesus. The Gospel of Grace brings the blessings of God in our lives.

"All who rely on observing the law are under a curse, for it is written: 'Cursed is everyone who does not continue to do everything written in the Book of the Law'" (Galatians 3:10).

If we rely on observing the law to be made righteous, we are under a curse. Did you see that? These are pretty strong words. This scripture cannot be any clearer. However, if we receive God's grace to be made righteous rather than thinking we can make ourselves righteous by observing the law, the curse is destroyed over our life and the blessings of God are released to us.

> *"And it shall come to pass, if thou shalt hearken dili-gently unto the voice of the Lord thy God, to observe and to do all his commandments which I command thee this day, that the Lord thy God will set thee on high above all nations of the earth. And all these blessings shall come on thee, and overtake thee, if thou shalt hearken unto the voice of the Lord thy God"* (Deuteronomy 28:1-2, KJV, emphasis added).

I read somewhere or heard someone say that the blessings of God will chase after you and overtake you. I like that. I declare that the blessings of God are chasing after me and overtaking me and my family.

In Deuteronomy 28:1 it says "If". If you listen to God and observe all His commandments these blessings will come upon you. This word "if" is making a qualification. Have you done all these things? If so, you are entitled to all these blessings. I would say to you that you can't fully obey all of the ten commandments, but Jesus has fully obeyed for you (in your place). **In Christ Jesus**, you have fully obeyed all God's commands. Because Jesus did it for you, you can confidently receive all His blessings. This is your inheritance in Christ Jesus. He has given you everything. His divine power, His grace, His righteousness, His holiness and everything that was His is now yours. He left you every-thing when He wrote His Last Will and Testament. You become the beneficiary of His whole estate when you believe.

It is because of Jesus that we have these blessings in Deuteronomy Chapter 28. It is because He has fully obeyed for us. Jesus has made the difference.

I would encourage you to read Deuteronomy 28:3-13 for yourself to see the blessings that you now have as a child of God. Declare them over your life and your loved ones.

*"Grace and peace be yours in abundance through the knowledge of God and of Jesus our Lord. His divine power has given us everything we need for life and godliness through our knowledge of him who called us by his own glory and goodness. Through these he has given us his very great and precious promises, so that through them you may participate in the **divine nature** and escape the corruption in the world caused by evil desires. For this very reason, make every effort to add to your faith goodness; and to goodness, knowledge; and to knowledge, self-control; and to self-control, perseverance; and to perseverance, godliness; and to godliness brotherly kindness; and to brotherly kindness, love. For if you possess these qualities in increasing measure, they will keep you from being ineffective and unproductive in your knowledge of our Lord Jesus Christ. But if anyone does not have them, he is nearsighted and blind, and **has forgotten that he has been cleansed from his past sins"** (2 Peter 1:2-9, emphasis added).*

When we know and **remember** that we have been cleansed from our sins, we will possess these qualities in increasing measure. If we **forget** what Jesus did for us, we become spiritually blind. If we try to develop these qualities in our own strength we become nearsighted. What this scripture is saying is that if we **remember** that our sins are forgiven, we will have **His divine nature** operating in and through us.

When we read scriptures like this from the viewpoint of the law rather than from the viewpoint of grace, we get loaded down with guilt and condemnation again. We think we have to produce all these qualities and when we can't we feel condemned. We become sin conscious again rather than righteous conscious. When we are sin conscious, it keeps us from being productive and producing these qualities in our life. It is His **divine nature** that already lives in us that produces these qualities in our lives, not our self-efforts. The **divine nature** is part of our inheritance in Christ Jesus.

Peter is saying that the reason why you don't have these qualities operating in your life – faith, godliness, etc. is because you have forgotten that you have been cleansed from all your sins and you have forgotten that the old sinful nature has been replaced with God's nature (the divine nature). I will elaborate more on the divine nature in the Chapter "What Did Jesus Circumcise You From?" Remember that your sins are all forgiven and as you remember, you will possess these qualities in increasing measure.

Can you see what a difference it makes when you look at this scripture this way?

Believers who are genuinely struggling with sin (whether it is addictions or the flesh) and can't get the victory but want it, and are crying out to God to set them free, God says His grace and His gift of righteousness are available to you today. You only have to receive them. Stop struggling in your flesh. You can't set yourself free from sin or addictions, but Christ can and has. Stop looking at yourself, your sin, your shortcomings and start looking at Jesus and who you are in Christ and declaring His promises over your life. Of course, you have to want to be free. Believe in Jesus' finished work and be righteousness conscious. Keep studying, meditating upon and feeding on the Gospel of Grace so that your mind is renewed and so that you can see yourself free and walking in victory. Grace will transform you from the inside out.

When I started to understand grace in my life (after many years of believing in Jesus) by reading a Book by a well-known Pastor, I could not believe that all my sins (past, present and future sins) were forgiven without me confessing them. The one scripture that came to my mind immediately when I was reading this Book was 1 John 1:9. I kept thinking that he would say something that would fit in with my theology that I needed to confess my sins in order to be forgiven and keep short accounts with God but he didn't.

When I began to read the New Testament, wanting to understand it through the lens of grace instead of the lens of the law, I would ask the Holy Spirit "what about this and what about that" and He began to help me see things in scripture that I had never understood before. It was so exciting when the Holy Spirit would teach me and turn my thinking right side up. For example, I mentioned 1 John 1:9 above.

John says in 1 John 1:9 that if we confess our sins He is faithful and just to forgive us of all our sins. I always understood this scripture to mean that I needed to confess my sins and then God would forgive me. However, in the first Chapter of 1 John, he was not even talking to believers, he was talking to Gnostics. Gnostics did not believe that Jesus came in the flesh. They did not believe in the existence of sin. They believed that the possession of knowledge was the only requirement for salvation. 1 John 1:9 was primarily a salvation verse. Gnostics were claiming to have fellowship with God in 1 John 1:6 because of their religious acts but they were really walking in darkness and did not have the truth. John tells them that if they would come to Jesus and walk in the light, they would have fellowship with other believers and Jesus would purify them from all sin. Paul was telling them that without Christ they were sinners and if they confessed their sin, Jesus was faithful and just and would forgive their sins and purify them from all unrighteousness. 1 John 1:9 was directed to Gnostics.

In 1 John 2:1, the very next Chapter, John addresses the believer. He starts to talk to believers and says if you sin, Jesus is your defense and has atoned for your sins. He does not tell the believer to confess their sins like he did the Gnostics but rather he says that their sins are already atoned for. In other words, he tells the believer to receive forgiveness of their sins.

Now don't misunderstand what I am saying. There is nothing wrong with confessing your sins and telling God you are sorry for your sins. However, when you do this, receive God's forgiveness right away. I believe that my sins are forgiven even without confessing them. Besides it is not possible to confess every sin we commit. There may be some sins we are committing that we aren't even consciously aware of. If we are constantly confessing our sins, we become sin conscious instead of righteousness conscious. It puts our focus on ourselves and on our sin instead of on Jesus which is where I want my focus to be. Even when we sin, we are still the righteousness of God in Christ Jesus because His righteousness was given to us as a gift.

"Now I commit you to the word of his grace which can build you up and give you an inheritance among all those who are sanctified" (Acts 20:32).

Paul was giving a farewell speech because he knew that he was going to Jerusalem not knowing what would happen to him there. He was committing the Ephesian elders to the word of God's grace. **He said that grace, if you let it, will build you up and give you an inheritance among the sanctified.** You are sanctified in Christ Jesus. Grace will build you up. Grace will encourage you in the most holy faith. Grace will strengthen you and keep you.

When we read the Bible, we need to look at who is talking, who the writer is talking to, what the time frame was (before the cross or after the cross) and to look at the whole context rather than isolated verses. Scripture will interpret scripture. Read the scriptures surrounding the verse so that you will see the context leading up to it or after it.

My friend, we can read the Bible from the viewpoint of the law or we can read the Bible from the viewpoint of grace. Start seeing God's grace when you read the Bible which brings life and freedom rather than seeing the law which brings bondage, sin, condemnation and death. Ask God, through His Spirit, to give you the spirit of wisdom and revelation to understand His grace. Start receiving His grace and His gift of righteousness to reign in life over negative emotions, addictions, sin, etc.

Now in this Book, I am talking to believers who genuinely want to be free from sin and who want God's grace to set them free not those who are looking for an excuse to remain in their sin and justify their actions. Those who deliberately want to remain and continue in their sin with no intention or desire to turn from it (those who are **not** trusting in God's grace to help them overcome sin) have fallen from grace back into **worldly** living. The Bible says that we, as believers, are in the **world** but not to be of the **world**. (see John 15:19, 17:6, 14, 15, 16, Romans 12:2, 1 Corinthians 2:12 and Galatians 6:14) God does not want us to have one foot in the Kingdom of God and one foot in the world because that is a very dangerous, unfruitful and unrewarding place to be. He also does not want us to have one foot in religion (self-righteousness) and one foot in the Kingdom of God as that also is a very dangerous, unfruitful and unrewarding place to be. God wants us to have both feet firmly planted in the Kingdom of God for this is where we will be fruitful, victorious, overcoming and conquering saints who will receive many rewards in heaven.

When believers **insist** on remaining in their sin (living a worldly lifestyle), their heart becomes hardened by sin's deceitfulness and they are in danger of losing their salvation by no longer believing in Jesus. Since the Bible says we are saved by believing in Jesus **with our heart** (not head knowledge of Jesus), we need to continue to believe in Him to the very end in order to have salvation. Colossians 1:22-23 says "But now he has reconciled you by Christ's physical body through death to present you holy in his sight, without blemish and free from accusation—, **if you continue in your faith**, established and firm, not moved from the hope held out in the gospel."

However, if you desire to be free from sin and you are receiving God's grace and gift of righteousness to help you to reign over that sin (trusting God to set you free) you are right with God because you believe in Jesus with your heart. Continue to live in Him so that your mind is renewed with the Word of God and grow up in your salvation now that you have tasted that the Lord is good.

Knowing What Jesus' Circumcised You From Brings Joy

Do you know that because of Adam's sin, everyone born into this world is born with a sinful nature/flesh that cannot please God even though at birth we had not sinned ourselves? We know that Adam & Eve sinned against God when they ate of the fruit of the tree in the garden that God told them not to eat of. God made everything in the garden for Adam and Eve to enjoy. The only command that God gave to them was to not eat of the fruit of the tree of the knowledge of good and evil or they would surely die (see Genesis 2:16). Well, we know that Adam & Eve ate of that fruit and did not die physically but they did die spiritually. Their spirit died the day they ate of the fruit and everyone born after them was born with a sinful nature/flesh and spiritually dead.

I'm going to show you a scripture that says that when we are born into this world, our spirit is dead to God because of Adam's sin but when we believe in Jesus, we are made alive to God. We are born again referring to a spiritual birth.

> *"For if, by the trespass (sin) of the one man (Adam),* ***death*** *reigned through that one man (Adam), how much more will those who* ***receive*** *God's abundant provision of grace (unearned, unmerited, undeserved favor of God) and of the gift of righteousness reign (or rule) in* ***life*** *through the one man, Jesus Christ.*

> *Consequently, just as the result of one trespass (sin) was condemnation for all men, so also the result of one act of righteousness (by Jesus) was justification that brings **life** for all men. For just as through the disobedience of the one man (Adam) the many were **made sinners**, so also through the obedience of the one man (Jesus) all men will be **made righteous** (made right with God; being restored to a right relationship with God)" (Romans 5:17-19, emphasis and parenthesis added).*

Over the years I have heard a lot of preaching and teaching on the sinful nature and the flesh. I was taught that they are separate. I was taught that the sinful nature was dealt with when I accepted Jesus as my Savior and Lord but that I still have a flesh to contend with. However, in studying the scriptures, I believe the sinful nature and the flesh are the same. It would be very unlike God to set us free from the sinful nature and leave us to struggle with the flesh.

I looked up the word "flesh" in the Strong's Exhaustive Concordance and it says: human nature with all its frailties and passions. Carnally minded.

This sure sounds like the sinful nature to me. I believe the flesh is the sinful nature and the sinful nature is the flesh. We have tried to separate them but I don't believe they should be separated. If you believe they are separate, it leaves you with a wrong mindset that you still have a flesh to fight. The Bible says that **your fight is the good fight of faith**. Instead of fighting your flesh, you need to fight the good fight of faith to believe the truth of God's Word that the flesh or sinful nature or old man is dead (I believe these are all the same) and that Jesus has already set you free. **Your sinful nature has been replaced with God's very own nature**. When you sin, it takes faith to believe this and that is why it is called the good fight of faith. **It is a fight to believe that your sinful nature/flesh/old man is dead when you sin, and faith to believe that you have God's nature operating in you now.** What is God's nature? His nature is love.

*"Be imitators of God, therefore, as dearly loved children and **live a life of love** just as Christ loved us and gave himself up for us as a fragrant offering and sacrifice to God" (Ephesians 5:1-2, emphasis added).*

If we love as Christ loved us, we will not enter into the things of the flesh. In order to love as Christ loved us, our minds need to be renewed with the Word of God that God loves us unconditionally. As we are permeated with His love, it will flow out of us effortlessly.

If you struggle to get rid of the sin in your life that means you are struggling with all your self-efforts to set yourself free. In other words, you can do it yourself. You don't need Jesus. What you need to do is to **believe** that Jesus has set you free from the sinful nature, your flesh, the old man and receive His nature (His unconditional love and grace) and every time you fail to keep receiving His love and grace. Meditate on God's grace, feed on His love, His goodness, His righteousness, etc. and sin will lose its power over you and one day you will realize you are free. Can you see the difference this will make?

Let me back this up with scripture.

Paul says in Romans 7:14-25 "We know that the law is spiritual; but I am unspiritual, sold as a slave to sin. I do not understand what I do. For what I want to do I do not do, but what I hate I do. And if I do what I do not want to do, I agree that the law is good. As it is, it is no longer I myself who do it, but it is sin living in me. I know that nothing good lives in me, that is, in my sinful nature. For I have the desire to do what is good, but I cannot carry it out. For what I do is not the good I want to do, no, the evil I do not want to do—this I keep on doing. Now if I do what I do not want to do, it is no longer I who do it, but it is sin living in me that does it. So I find this law at work: When I want to do good, evil is right there with me. For in my inner being I delight in God's law; but I see another law at work in the members of my body, waging war against the law of my mind and making me a prisoner of the law of sin at work within my members. What a wretched man I am! Who will rescue me from **this body of death?** Thanks be to God — through Jesus Christ our Lord!"

Paul was a Pharisee and according to his upbringing was blame-less, yet the very law he trusted in still condemned him **before he was a Christian**. Paul is talking about himself dealing with his flesh **prior to his salvation**, while he was still living under the law, still having the sinful nature. Paul was speaking of himself not in the context of being a Christian but in the context of his life prior to being a Christian. In Philippians 3:1-9 Paul says that when he was walking under the law he put confidence in the flesh thinking that the law would bring righteousness but found out that only grace can produce true righteousness by faith. Paul says in verse 14 above "I am unspiritual", yet we know that Paul was alive to God **after sal-vation**. He had the nature of God in him. He could not be unspiritual since he was now born again. He goes on to say that he was sold as a slave to sin. This was true of Paul's life prior to salvation but not after. In 1 Corinthians 15:31 Paul says that he dies every day. He counts himself dead to sin and alive to God every day. He remem-bers what Jesus did for him every day. In verse18 above Paul says that he knows that nothing good lives in him, that is in his sinful fleshly nature. First of all, we know that Jesus lived in Paul and Jesus is good, so something good did live in Paul but not before salvation. Secondly, according to Galatians 2:20, Paul's sinful fleshly nature was crucified with Christ and it no longer lived in him but Christ lived in him. In verse 24 above he says "What a wretched man I am!". This was true of Paul's life prior to salvation but not after. He goes on to ask a question "Who will rescue me from **this body of death?**". Then he gives the answer in verse 25 above "Thanks be to God – through Jesus Christ our Lord!". He says that Jesus rescued him. Paul was saying that he could not rescue himself from the law or from the sinful fleshly nature but he says that Jesus Christ can and will rescue everyone who comes to Him. When you believe in Jesus, you are a new creature. The old is gone and the new has come (see 2 Corinthians 5:17).

Since Paul was in Christ when he wrote this, since he was already crucified with Christ, the sinful fleshly nature was no longer alive in him. He was dead to sin and alive to God. Paul was not talking about himself as a Christian struggling with his flesh but rather he was giving us a picture of the struggles he had trying to obey the law without Christ in his life. That's self-righteousness. God does not accept self-righteousness. Besides, we cannot fully obey the law. We will never be made righteous by trying to obey the law. We cannot earn the righteousness that God accepts from trying to obey the law.

Believers often struggle to try to obey the law in order to become more righteous. We need to stop this. The moment we believed in Jesus, He gave us His very own righteousness. We are as righteous as Jesus is. We cannot become anymore righteous. When Jesus gave us His righteousness, it was a gift. We could not earn it. Jesus fully obeyed the law for believers because we could not fully obey it ourselves.

> *"In whom also ye are* **circumcised** *with the circumcision made without hands, in putting off* **the body of the sins of the flesh** *by the circumcision of Christ"* *(Colossians 2:11, KJV, emphasis added).*

This scripture says that Jesus circumcised us from the body of the sins of the flesh. What is **the body of the sins of the flesh** that Jesus circumcised us from? This is what the Holy Spirit showed me. He said **the body of the sins of the flesh is the law**. The law is the body that causes us to sin and reveals to us that we are sinners in need of a Savior. Jesus removed the body or the law from us who believe. He circumcised us from the body, the law, by nailing it to the cross. By circumcising us from the law, He cut away the sinful fleshly nature from us and replaced it with His very own nature. Only in Christ are we circumcised from the law thus also being circumcised from our sinful fleshly nature and given God's very own nature in its place.

Remember in Romans 7:24 I read "What a wretched man I am! Who will rescue me from **this body of death?**".

What is this **body of death** that Paul was referring to? It is the same as the **body of the sins of the flesh** that we just talked about in Colossians 2:11. The body of the sins of the flesh and the body of death are the same. Remember the body of the sins of the flesh is the law. Therefore the body of death is also the law. The law is the body that causes people to sin and it brings death. Paul, talking about himself prior to salvation, is saying who will rescue me from the law.

Paul says, Jesus will rescue me and infers that Jesus will rescue all who come to Him.

> *"Now if we died with Christ, we believe that we will also live with him. For we know that since Christ was raised from the dead, he cannot die again; death no longer has mastery over him. The death he died, he died to sin **once for all**; but the life he lives, he lives to God. In the same way, (Christ only died to sin one time) count yourselves dead to sin but alive to God in Christ Jesus. Therefore do not let sin reign in your mortal body so that you obey its evil desires. Do not offer the parts of your body to sin, as instruments of wickedness, but rather offer yourselves to God, as those who have been brought from death to life (**once for all time**); and offer the parts of your body to him as instruments of righteousness. For sin shall not be your master, because you are not under the law, but under grace" (Romans 6:8-14, emphasis and parenthesis added).*

You need to grasp this truth that Jesus has circumcised you from the law and the sinful/fleshly nature/old man and, therefore, you are dead to sin and alive to God **once for all**. You need to grasp that sin is no longer your master because you are no longer under the law but under grace (unmerited, unearned, undeserved favor of God). **You believe this by faith**. It may not be a manifested reality in your everyday life but you are to walk by faith, not by sight. This is why it is called "faith". If you sin and you want to be free from that sin, don't condemn yourself. Instead remember that because you are no longer under the law, sin has no dominion or control over you. In other words, Jesus has set you free. Whom the Son sets free is free indeed. Remember that you now have God's very own nature in you. Focus on the truth that you now have the divine nature in you which replaced your sinful/fleshly nature. Meditate on this until the divine nature takes predominance in your life. Remember that your sinful nature/fleshly nature/old man has been crucified with Christ and it no longer lives in you but Christ lives in you and the life you now live you live by the faith of the Son of God who died for you (see Galatians 2:20). Declare this over yourself by faith. Remember and declare that you are the righteousness of God in Christ Jesus. As you do this, strongholds are being pulled down in your life and your mind is being renewed with the Word of God. Keep focusing on who you now are in Christ and not on your sorrow, sin, etc. and you will realize one day that you are free.

Pray and offer yourself to God as one who has been brought from death to life and offer the parts of your body to Him as instruments of righteousness. You do this by faith. Go ahead and do that now. Offer yourself to God as Romans 6:13 above instructs.

> *"When you **were** dead in your sins and in the uncircumcision of your sinful nature, God made you **alive** with Christ. He forgave us all our sins, having canceled the written code (the law), with its regulations, that was against us and that stood opposed to us; he took it away, nailing it to the cross" (Colossians 2:13-14, emphasis and parenthesis added).*

This scripture says "when you **were dead** in your sins". Did you notice that this is past tense? Before you came to Christ, you were dead in your sins and your nature was sinful or fleshly but now because you believe in Jesus, you are **alive** in Him and have His nature. This is present tense. Jesus forgave you of all your sins. He gave you His nature. Wow! You need to see yourself alive in Christ, having His nature and completely forgiven. He nailed the law (which is the written code) to the cross and freed everyone who would believe in Him from the law and from the sinful fleshly nature. The law was put into effect by God Himself so that each person, apart from Christ, would recognize that they are sinners in need of a Savior and that Savior is Jesus who is God in the flesh. Therefore, the law is good and intended to lead you to Christ, but once you believe, you are no longer under the supervision of the law.

Read what Paul says in the following scripture.

*"Not that I have already obtained all this, or have already been made perfect, but I press on to take hold of that for which Christ Jesus took hold of me. Brothers, I do not consider myself yet to have taken hold of it. But one thing I do: **Forgetting what is behind and straining toward what is ahead**, I press on toward the goal to win the prize for which God has called me heavenward in Christ Jesus" (Philippians 3:12-14, emphasis added).*

This is what we need to do. In our imperfect state, we press on to take hold of (grasp firmly) that which Christ Jesus accomplished for us in His redemptive work. Forget the past. We can't change the past but by believing right our future will be changed.

We can see Paul running this race just like an Olympic runner. He was passionate about running this race well and finishing this race well. Paul pressed forward with all Jesus' strength working in him to complete the race. It was not in his own strength. The prize for completing the race was to one day be with Jesus forever. Paul was following Christ with an intensity as he was determined to get the prize. He did this by keeping his eyes on Jesus. He could not run this race and win any other way. It was because he was keeping his eyes on Jesus, the prize, that gave him the strength to keep pressing on towards the mark. He was pursuing Christ actively each and every day of his life. We need to follow Paul's example as we run our race so that we too will remain in Jesus (believe in Him) to the very end and win the prize.

"If the ministry that condemns men is glorious, how much more glorious is the ministry that brings righteousness" (2 Corinthians 3:9).

God used the law to bring us to Christ. Paul says the ministry of the law which brings condemnation is glorious but then he says **how much more glorious is the ministry that brings righteousness**. The ministry that brings righteousness is the message of grace. The message or ministry of grace is much more glorious than the ministry of the law because the law condemns but grace frees us to live a righteous and godly life style. Under the law, self-righteous-ness springs forth but grace will spring forth Christ's righteousness in us. Believing with our heart that we are the righteousness of God in Christ Jesus is a **weapon** that we use against the enemy when he tries to bring condemnation. Paul says in 2 Corinthians 6:7 that he had **weapons of righteousness** in his right hand and in the left. I never saw this before. Let's look at this scripture.

"By [speaking] the word of truth, in the power of God, with the **weapons of righteousness** *for the right hand [to attack] and for the left hand [to defend]" (2 Corinthians 6:7, Amplified, emphasis added).*

He had the **weapons** of righteousness in both his hands. He was wielding the truth that he is the righteousness of God in Christ Jesus as a **double**-edged sword in both his hands. We need to have the weapons of righteousness in both our hands as well. Did you notice that the word "weapons" is pluralized? This weapon is two-fold. It is used to attack our enemy and to defend ourselves. Righteousness is a weapon we use against the enemy of our soul and to declare who we are in Christ Jesus.

1 Corinthians 15:56b says that the **power of sin is the law**. Did you see that? The power of sin is the law. The law strengthens sin. It is the law that reveals to people that they are sinners. Grace reveals our righteousness.

If we insist on living under the law to be made righteous, we resurrect and give strength to the sinful fleshly nature/old man but if we embrace the grace of God, the sinful fleshly nature/old man has no power over us and we are freed to express **God's nature**. The **nature of God** is the fruit of the Spirit (the fruit of righteousness that we talked about earlier in this Book): love which will bring forth joy, peace, patience, kindness, goodness, gentleness, faithfulness and self-control. This is the nature we are now walking in **by faith** because we walk in the grace of God and because we now have the weapons of righteousness in both our hands. This fruit is in us already. We need to allow the fruit of righteousness to arise within us and flow out of us **by faith**. The Passion Translation of Galatians 5:22-23 says "But the fruit produced by the Holy Spirit within you is divine love in all its various expressions. This love is revealed through: joy that overflows, peace that subdues, patience that endures, kindness in action, a life full of virtue, faith that prevails, gentleness of heart, and strength of spirit." A note in The Passion Translation says "There is clear textual inference that the fruit (singular) of the Holy Spirit is love with the other virtues displaying aspects of the greatest quality of Spirit-life, agape love."

When we come to Christ Jesus, our sinful nature/flesh/old man is crucified. Years ago I read a child's Book to my grandson. In this Book was a picture of a little boy hanging on the tree with Jesus. This little boy was hanging in front of Jesus with his arms stretched over Jesus' arms and his little body stretched over Jesus' heart. Picture yourself hanging on the tree with Jesus. Picture your old man, your old sinful nature, your flesh hanging there crucified with Him. This is what actually happened in the spirit realm when you first believed. Now you need to apply this, **by grace through faith**, to your everyday living. In other words, when you find yourself doing something wrong, you need to remember that Jesus circumcised you from the old man. Remember that the old man is dead and is no longer alive. Remember that you now have **God's nature** in you. This will empower you to say "no" to ungodliness and "yes" to godliness.

In the Old Testament God gave Abraham the covenant of circumcision. What was this circumcision?

Let's look at Genesis 17:9-14 "Then God said to Abraham, "As for you, you must keep my covenant, you and your descendants after you for the generations to come. This is my covenant with you and your descendants after you, the covenant you are to keep: Every male among you shall be circumcised. You are to undergo circumcision, and it will be the **sign of the covenant between me and you**. For the generations to come every male among you who is eight days old must be circumcised, including those born in your household or bought with money from a foreigner – those who are not your offspring. Whether born in your household or bought with your money, they must be circumcised. My covenant **in your flesh** is to be an everlasting covenant. Any uncircumcised male, who has not been circumcised **in the flesh,** will be cut off from his people, he has broken my covenant."

Circumcision means to cut off the foreskin which is a piece of flesh.

The sign of the covenant that God made with Abraham and his descendants was circumcision which was a cutting away of the foreskin (flesh) of every male. This was the sign that they were God's children. **The sign of the covenant of grace that God has made with every believer today is a spiritual cutting away of the law thus cutting away the flesh which is the sinful nature and also referred to as the "old man".** This takes place the instant we believe in Jesus as our Savior and Lord and enter into a covenant with Him. Remember in Colossians 2:11 it says "In whom also ye are circumcised with the circumcision made without hands, in putting off the body of the sins of the flesh by the circumcision of Christ." This isn't something that we can do. Only Christ can do this and He does it the moment we believe in Him. It is a supernatural cutting away done by God Himself, not by our own self-efforts and not by the hands of man. Therefore, when we are tempted to sin, we need to remember that Jesus has circumcised us from the law which strengthens sin and He has cut away the sinful fleshly nature/the old man and replaced it with His nature which is love. **This understanding will empower us to walk delivered from the flesh.** Does that mean we will never sin again? Absolutely not but when we do it will give us ammunition to walk in the victory that Jesus has already given to us.

> *"Since, then, you have been raised with Christ, **set your hearts** on things above, where Christ is, seated at the right hand of God. **Set your minds** on things above, not on earthly things. **For you died,** and your life is now hidden with Christ in God. When Christ, who is your life, appears, then you also will appear with him in glory. Put to death, therefore, whatever belongs to your earthly nature: sexual immorality, impurity, lust, evil desires and greed, which is idolatry. Because of these, the wrath of God is coming. You used to walk in these ways, in the life you once lived (past tense). But now you must rid yourselves of all*

such things as these: anger, rage, malice, slander, and filthy language from your lips. Do not lie to each other, since you have taken off your old self with its practices (past tense) and have put on (present tense) the new self, which is being renewed in knowledge in the image of its Creator" (Colossians 3:1-10, emphasis and parenthesis added).

We need to use our faith to recognize and believe that the old man, the old self, the sinful fleshly nature is dead/circumcised and that we are alive in Christ. This is a finished work. Our minds need to be renewed with this truth. Paul says not to resurrect the old sinful fleshly man by putting your attention on earthly things. I believe this is the point that Paul is making in this scripture. He names a bunch of sins that in coming to Christ the Colossians had overcome but perhaps were resurrecting and walking in some of them again because they did not have the understanding that their old man was crucified with Christ. He instructs the Colossians to put them to death for this is worldly living. How do they do this? Paul gives them the answer. He reminds them that they died with Christ. He reminds them to put their attention on Christ and things above. He says set your hearts/minds on things above, where Christ is, seated at the right hand of God. Know that you are seated there as a co-heir with Christ. **Consider** where you are seated. **Consider** that you have been circumcised from the law and you have also been circumcised from the sinful fleshly nature. **Consider** that you now have God's nature. Think about these things for what we dwell on, we will do. Think about what you are thinking about. Sin is conceived. It doesn't just happen. It is first **thought** about and **considered**. When the thoughts or temptations come, don't consider them. We cannot be tempted with things we don't think about. Say "No, my sinful fleshly nature has been crucified with Christ and it no longer lives in me but Christ lives in me. His nature now lives in me and the life I live in this body I live by the faith of the Son of God who loved me and gave himself for me". **Consider** that you have been made new. By **considering** how God now sees you, your mind is being renewed with the knowledge of God and transformation is taking place on the inside of you. When you get filled up with God's Word and who you are in Christ, the transformation that begins on the inside of you will break out of you.

I cannot emphasize enough how very important this is for us, as Christians, to understand so that we are not controlled by the sinful fleshly nature/old man but rather know that Christ has circumcised us from the law and the sinful fleshly nature/old man. We are a new creation in Christ Jesus and we have His divine nature. We are no longer under law but under grace. **When we live under grace, we are favored with the ability to go and sin no more.** It will cause us to reign over sin. Sin no longer has dominion over us. When we understand the love of God for us, that He forgave us of all our sins (past, present and future sins), this should set us free from ever wanting to sin again not make us **think** that we can go and do whatever we want to. That's wrong **thinking**. That kind of **thinking** will conceive sin.

Prayer: Father, please help my thinking/believing to be right so that right actions will follow, in Jesus' Name.

> *"Therefore, as God's chosen people, holy and dearly loved, clothe yourselves with compassion, kindness, humility, gentleness and patience. Bear with each other and forgive whatever grievances you may have against one another. Forgive as the Lord forgave you. And over all these virtues put on love, which binds them all together in perfect unity. Let the peace of Christ rule in your hearts, since as members of one body you were called to peace. And be thankful. Let the word of Christ dwell in you richly" (Colossians 3:12-16a).*

This is God's Will for our lives. If we are born again, we have God's nature on the inside of us. As we focus on Jesus and His nature, we will live a victorious life in Christ. As we get our minds renewed with the truth of God's Word, we will live clothed with compassion, kindness, humility, etc. more and more. None of us are perfect. We are all learning and growing in Christ Jesus day by day.

"You, however, are controlled not by the sinful nature, but by the Spirit if the Spirit of God lives in you" (Romans 8:9).

Do you have the Spirit of God living in you? Every born again believer has the Spirit of God living in them. This scripture says that if the Spirit of God lives in you, you are controlled not by the sinful fleshly nature but **by the Spirit**. It is the power of the Spirit living in you that will enable you to say "no" to ungodliness and "yes" to God. God has supplied everything you need for life and godliness. You need to believe this even when you make wrong choices because it is the renewing of your mind with the truth that will set you free and eventually the wrong choices will turn into right choices. Don't condemn yourself. Don't be so hard on yourself. You can't fix the sin problem in your life but Jesus can and, in fact, has already set you free from the law which is the power of sin, if you are a believer. You just have to renew your mind with the Word of God and when you believe right, you will live right.

"Do not be misled: Bad company corrupts good character" (1 Corinthians 15:33).

KJV says in verse 34a "**Awake to righteousness** and sin not."
This scripture says to wake up to the truth that you now have Jesus' righteousness, wake up to the truth that you are as righteous as Jesus is and you will stop sinning. Paul also gives some practical advice. He says bad company corrupts good character. You may need to separate yourself from friends who are leading you astray. I had to do this myself.

*"There is therefore now **no condemnation** for those who are **in Christ Jesus**. For the law of the Spirit of life in Christ Jesus has set you free from the law of sin and of death. For what the Law could not do, weak as it was through the flesh, **God did**: sending His own Son in the likeness of sinful flesh and as an offering for sin, He condemned sin in the flesh, in order that the*

> *requirement of the Law might be fulfilled in us, **who***
> ***do not walk according to the flesh, but according to***
> ***the Spirit***" *(Romans 8:1-4, NAS, emphasis added).*

When we live according to the Spirit by remembering that our sins are forgiven, that we are saved by grace through faith in Jesus Christ, that we are the righteousness of God in Christ Jesus, that we have been circumcised from the law and from the sinful fleshly nature/old man, that we are alive to God and have His very own nature, the flesh has no power over us. By believing this we are living according to the Spirit. We are no longer living according to the flesh.

> *"For if you live according to the sinful nature, you will*
> *die; but if **by the Spirit** you put to death the misdeeds*
> *of the body, you will live because those who are led*
> *by the Spirit of God are sons of God"* *(Romans 8:13-*
> *14, emphasis added).*

Did you see that? It says that it is **by the Spirit** that you put to death the misdeeds of the body not by your own self-efforts. If you focus on your sinful fleshly nature, **you will resurrect that nature** and you will die but if you focus on the Spirit you will live. You need to think about what you are focusing on. Don't focus on your sins. This will not set you free. Rather focus on the Spirit. Listen to Him and He will direct you in accordance with God's Word. Focus on the love of God for you. Focus on the grace of God for you personally. Focus on scriptures that will build you up and encourage you. Focus on the truth that you are valued by God, that you are the apple of His eye, that you are His treasured possession and that you are chosen by God. Find scriptures that will bring healing to your heart and meditate on them. These truths will set you free and establish you on a right course that leads to a lifestyle of godliness.

Prayer: Holy Spirit I ask you to take control of my mind. Please lead me into all truth. I want to be led by You.

Walking On Water Brings Joy

When Peter kept his eyes on Jesus, he walked on water. It was only when he allowed the distractions around him to take his eyes off Jesus that he began to sink. Then he cried out to Jesus and Jesus pulled him out of the water.

Let's look at the scripture about Peter walking on water.

"Immediately Jesus made the disciples get into the boat and go on ahead of him to the other side, while he dismissed the crowd. After he had dismissed them, he went up on a mountain side by himself to pray. When evening came, he was there alone, but the boat was already a considerable distance from land, **buffeted by the waves because the wind was against it***. During the fourth watch of the night Jesus went out to them,* **walking** *on the lake. When the disciples saw him walking on the lake, they were terrified. "It's a ghost," they said, and cried out in fear. But Jesus immediately said to them:* **"Take courage! It is I. Don't be afraid.***" "Lord, if it's you," Peter replied, tell me to come to you on the water." "Come," he said. Then Peter got down out of the boat, walked on the water and came toward Jesus. But* **when he saw the wind he was afraid** *and, beginning to sink, cried out, "Lord, save me!" Immediately Jesus reached out*

his hand and caught him. "You of little faith", he said,
"Why did you doubt?" And when they climbed into
the boat, the wind died down" (Matthew 14:22-32,
emphasis added).

The disciples had seen Jesus perform many miracles but they had never seen Jesus walk on water before. This was something new to them. They did not know that it was Jesus until Jesus told them it was He. Jesus immediately told them not to fear but to take courage. So Peter said "If it is you Lord, tell me to come to you on the water." Peter was not completely convinced that it was Jesus because he said "*If* it is you, Lord". When Jesus told Peter to come, Peter then knew it was Jesus and **looking at Jesus**, he got out of the boat and walked on water. Wow! Peter walking on water. Was he even aware that he was walking on water? Was he so totally focused on Jesus that he did not even know that he was walking on water? Peter must have been completely oblivious to the wind and the waves because he was so focused on Jesus. But then the scripture says that he saw the wind and became afraid and began to sink. Now we know from this scripture that the boat was buffeted by the waves because the wind was against it. We know that the winds were strong and the waves high, yet Peter walked on those boisterous waves because he had his focus on Jesus. But then Peter took his focus off of Jesus and began to focus on the waves and the wind which were **the circumstances around him** and **he became afraid**, even though Jesus had just told him not to be afraid but to take courage.

How often have we done the same thing? I know I have.

I think the main thing that God wants us to learn from this passage is not walking on water but to not be afraid of our circumstances and to take courage in Him. He wants us to keep our eyes on Him and not on the circumstances in our lives.

The disciples thought Jesus was a ghost. The word "ghost" means a deceptive likeness or apparition. At that time in history, an apparition by night was a superstition among all nations. To sailors it was a sign of shipwreck. Jesus knew that when the disciples saw Him they would immediately think this and become fearful so He wanted to put their fears at rest right away by letting them know it was, in fact, Him and not an apparition. He wanted to let them know that He was there with them. When he said to Peter "You of little faith. Why did you doubt?", he was saying I told you it was me. **How can you be afraid when I am with you?** I am here Peter. I am with you. You saw the miracles that I did. How can you doubt when I am with you? Peter was acting like Jesus wasn't there with him. We act like that sometimes too.

When we are afraid, we are acting like Jesus is not with us. The Bible says He is in me and I am in Him. We are one. If we are believers in Jesus, we can't get any closer to Him than we already are. Jesus wants us to put our focus on Him who never leaves us nor forsakes us. Jesus is in us. Let us act like He is in us. When we act like He is in us, we will walk on water which is symbolic of us walking on our circumstances. What are your circumstances? What are my circumstances? Are we walking on them? Sometimes "Yes". Sometimes "No". The circumstances that Peter became fearful of were the boisterous waves and water that he was actually walking on. The wind was blowing and the waves were pounding before Peter got out of the boat. Yet he got out of the boat and walked on his circumstances because he had his focus on Jesus. We too can walk on our circumstances when we put our eyes on Jesus. When we put our eyes on Jesus, our circumstances will be under our feet just like the water was under Peter's feet. We are not to let the circumstances in our life distract us from focusing on Jesus and who He is and cause us to sink. No No No! Jesus tells us to look at Him and we will walk on top of our circumstances. Our circumstances should be under our feet. This doesn't mean that our circumstances have disappeared. The wind and waves were still all around Peter when he walked on water. It simply means that we are not focusing on them but on Jesus. As long as we are focusing on Jesus, our circumstances will not drown us.

I need this message as much as you do. I am paying attention myself as I write this, so that I can walk on water just like Peter did. There are circumstances in my life that I need to walk on and the way I can walk on them is to keep my eyes on Jesus. I need to be reminded of this continually as there are always new circumstances arising in my life. What about you?

I would like to share something with you. One day I was declaring God's promises as the flu was trying to come on my body. The flu was going around and people were sick up to a week with the flu. Although I did not feel well for about 9 to 10 hours, it was not able to take root in my body. I was determined to believe God's Word and to keep declaring it over my body. By doing so, I was keeping my focus on Jesus and not on the flu that was trying very hard to take over. All of a sudden I felt better and I knew I had won the good fight of faith. God is faithful to watch over His Word. Then again about four days later, the enemy tried to put a cold virus on me. I started with a sore throat in the middle of the night. I spent time in the night declaring God's Word and looking to Jesus. I have come to realize that it must be dealt with as soon as I feel the slightest attack. It is very important to take the time to come against it with God's Word right away or it would take root and I would be sick for much longer. Throughout the day, I declared God's Word over and over again as there were some minor symptoms. I was determined to stand on God's Word with His faith and receive the finished work of Jesus. Again I woke up during the last part of the 2nd night and I spent time declaring God's Word, believing in the finished work of Jesus, listening to worship music which helped me to keep my focus on Jesus and then I fell asleep. When I woke up in the morning I instantly became aware that the Holy Spirit was right there with me and He let me know that He was standing tall in me and He was empowering me, strengthening me and encouraging me to fight the good fight of faith. He revealed to me that I was not alone. We were joined together and I could not be defeated as long as I kept my eyes on Jesus and not on my circumstances. The Bible says that out of His glorious riches He will strengthen me with power **through His Spirit** in my inner being **so that** Christ may dwell in my heart through faith (see Ephesians 3:16-17a). I have prayed this prayer many times and the Holy Spirit was making known to me that morning that He was strengthening me with power in my inner being so that I could continue to believe and stand on God's Word. It was Jesus' faith that was at work in me. Although that cold tried very hard to take root, it was not able to do so. Praise the Lord!!!!!

In Ephesians 1:19-22 it says that God raised Christ from the dead and seated Him at his right hand in the heavenly realms, far above all rule and authority, power and dominion, and every title that can be given, not only in the present age but also in the one to come. And **God placed all things under his feet**.

And in Ephesians 2:6 it says that God raised **us up** with Christ and seated **us** with Him in the heavenly realms in Christ Jesus.

Did you see that? Jesus is seated far above all rule and authority, power and dominion and every title that can be given, and since we are in Christ Jesus **we are also seated** far above all rule and authority, power and dominion and every title that can be given.

We have been seated above our circumstances. Our circumstances are beneath us. We need to remind ourselves of where we are seated. When we know where we are seated and believe it, we will walk on water by walking on our circumstances. Our circumstances should not be walking on us but we can walk on our circumstances. The way we walk on our circumstances is to keep our eyes focused on Jesus alone. We can't allow the enemy or our circumstances to distract us. We need to receive God's abundant provision of grace to keep our eyes on Jesus. We can't do this in our own power but as we depend on Jesus, looking to Jesus to keep our eyes fixed on Him, we will overcome all the distractions of the enemy. The wind and waves were a distraction to Peter. What are the distractions the enemy uses in your life? If you don't know what these distractions are, ask the Holy Spirit to reveal them to you. When you know what the distractions are, you can take authority over them and pray and ask Holy Spirit, by His grace, to help you walk on those distractions (circumstances) and to keep your eyes on Jesus.

I want to take you to Ephesians Chapters 2 and 3 for a few minutes and I will tie together what I am about to say with what I have already said. This will get a little deep here but stick with me and you will see something you may have never seen before. In Ephesians 2:11 to 3:11 Paul is saying how God made one new man out of two, meaning the Jews and Gentiles.

> *"But now in Christ Jesus you who once were far away*
> *(Gentiles) have been brought near through the blood*
> *of Christ. For he himself is our peace, who has made*
> *the two (Jews and Gentiles) one and has destroyed*
> *the barrier, the dividing wall of hostility (which is*
> *the law), by abolishing in his flesh the law with its*

> *commandments and regulations. His purpose was to*
> *create in himself **one new man** out of the two, thus*
> *making peace, and in this **one body** to reconcile **both***
> ***of them to God through the cross**, by which he put to*
> *death their hostility" (Ephesians 2:13-16, emphasis*
> *and parenthesis added).*

So we see that **in Christ**, there is no longer Jew and Gentile (two separate people). By destroying the wall of hostility (which is the law) **which divided** the Jews and Gentiles, He created in Himself **one new man** out of the two and brought peace between the Jews and Gentiles. Now this one new man consists of believing Jews and believing Gentiles.

> *"Surely you have heard about the **administration***
> *of **God's grace** that was given to me for you, **that***
> ***is the mystery** made known to me by revelation, as*
> *I have already written briefly" (Ephesians 3:2,*
> *emphasis added).*

What is the mystery Paul was referring to and the mystery that he had already briefly written about?

It says in this scripture that the mystery is the Gospel of Grace and **by the Grace of God**, the Jews and Gentiles are **made one** in the Spirit. The dividing wall of hostility (the law) had to be removed by the cross of Jesus Christ in order that the Gospel of Grace could be revealed. The mystery is that we, as believers in Jesus Christ, are no longer under the administrative system of the law. We are now guided by the administration of God's grace. Grace is unearned, undeserved, unmerited favor of God. We can no longer earn God's favor as if we were still under the law. God's grace is unearned and we have access to God's grace by believing in Jesus with our hearts and receiving God's grace whether we are a Jew or a Gentile.

Let's read that in Ephesians 3:6 "This mystery is that through the gospel the Gentiles are heirs together with Israel, members together of one body (the Church), and sharers together in the promise in Christ Jesus" (parenthesis added).

So we have established that the mystery that Paul was referring to is the Gospel of Grace and through this Grace, God has made both Jew and Gentile one in Christ Jesus by abolishing in His flesh the law. He removed the law which was the dividing wall of hostility between Jews and Gentiles and by doing this, He created one new man in Christ Jesus, one Body, the Church. **The Church was created**.

> *"His intent (purpose for doing this) was that now, (now that the Gospel of Grace has been revealed and both Jews and Gentiles are made one in Christ Jesus) through the church, (the church has now been formed, one new man, out of the two) the **manifold wisdom of God should be made known (to who) to the rulers and authorities in the heavenly realms**, according to his eternal purpose which he accomplished in Christ Jesus our Lord"* *(Ephesians 3:10-11, emphasis and parenthesis added).*

I never understood what the manifold wisdom of God was before but God enlightened my heart as I pressed in to understand it and this is what He revealed to me.

The word "manifold" in Webster's dictionary means "having **many** forms, parts, etc., being such in **many** ways. The Amplified Bible says "**many**-sided wisdom of God".

So now that Jesus has removed the law which was the dividing wall of hostility that stood between the Jews and Gentiles and brought peace between them and now that He has made us one new man, one body (the Church) in Christ Jesus by the grace of God this **manifold wisdom of God** that the Church is to make known **is the Word of God**. The scripture says now that grace has come and the Church has been created, we are to make known (declare) to the rulers and authorities (both good and evil) in the heavenly realms the many-sided wisdom of God (which is the Word of God). How do we do this? We are to believe, pray and declare God's Word. By believing, praying and declaring God's Word (His promises in His Word), the **angelic** rulers and authorities are being released by our prayers and declarations to minister the Word of God back to us. God says that He watches over

His Word to perform it or bring it to pass in our lives. When we speak His Word over our lives and our loved ones, the angelic rulers and authorities are immediately charged for action. Think about what is happening in the heavenly spiritual realm around and about us when we pray and declare God's Word. Much activity is released to angelic beings in an unseen realm to bring to pass in our lives the Word that we are declaring. It is God's intent, His purpose for the Church to make known the manifold wisdom of God.

We just talked about what happens in the unseen realm when the **angelic** rulers and authorities hear us praying and declaring God's Word. Now what happens when the **demonic** rulers and authorities hear us praying and declaring God's Word? When we pray and declare God's Word (His promises) the **demonic** rulers and authorities are **notified** that they are already defeated and under our feet and they no longer have any authority over us. When we use the Sword of the Spirit (the Word of God) that we talked about earlier in this Book, the enemy takes off as fast as he can because he has no defense against the Word of God. This is good news!

Now I will attempt to tie this together with what I said earlier about walking on water, on our circumstances. As the Church makes known the manifold wisdom of God to the rulers and authorities in the heavenly realms, which is the Word of God, by declaring God's promises, we are keeping our eyes on Jesus and we are walking on water, walking on our circumstances. **The key is to keep our eyes focused on Jesus by praying and declaring His promises, by keeping His promises in our hearts and coming out of our mouths**. As we pray and declare God's Word, **we are making known God's Word** (His manifold wisdom) to the rulers and authorities (both good and evil) and by so doing we are keeping our eyes on Jesus. The scripture says that **this is God's eternal purpose which He accomplished in Christ Jesus our Lord**.

Whatever circumstances we find ourselves in, we need to go to the Word of God and find out what God promises us regarding these circumstances and then begin to declare His promises and pray His Word. As we do this, we are keeping our eyes on Jesus, who is the Word of God, and we are keeping our eyes on what He promises us, rather than on the circumstances. When we do this, we will find ourselves walking on water just like Peter. Remember the circumstances in Peter's life were the boisterous waters and when Peter kept his eyes on Jesus, he walked on his circumstances. It will be the same with us. We will walk on our circumstances when we keep our eyes on Jesus and make known the manifold wisdom of God which is His Word to the rulers and authorities by praying and declaring God's promises. Remember that God's grace is undeserved, unearned, unmerited favor. When the enemy comes at you to condemn you, quote the Word that you are saved by grace through faith, quote the Word that Jesus has fulfilled the law perfectly for you, quote the Word that there is now no condemnation for those who are in Christ Jesus, quote the Word that you are the righteousness of God in Christ Jesus, quote the Word that your sins are all forgiven, quote the Word that Christ redeemed you from the curse of the law and the blessings of God are flowing in your life, etc. and a flurry of activity will take place in the heavenly realms. The angelic rulers will immediately come to your defense and the demonic rulers will take off. Praise the Lord!

This message that the Holy Spirit gave to me has helped me tremendously and continues to help me and I hope you are being helped as well. We all need to depend on God for the victory in our lives. Preachers and teachers are no different. We all have times of difficulty in our lives. I am so glad that the Holy Spirit gave me more ammunition from the Word of God that helps me on a day to day basis to walk on water. I hope that this teaching will help you walk on your water too, one day at a time.

In this Book, I have already mentioned many scriptures that we can pray and declare over ourselves and our loved ones. Now let's look at a few more scriptures that we can make known to the rulers and authorities in the heavenly realm by praying and declaring them, thereby walking on water, walking on our circumstances. I'm going to turn these scriptures into a prayer. You can pray this over yourself and for others as well.

1. Thank You Father, in Jesus' Name, I receive Your abundant provision of grace and your gift of righteousness to reign in life through Jesus Christ (see Romans 5:17b).

When we know we are reigning, the devil knows he is defeated. Thank God that your loved ones are receiving God's grace and gift of righteousness and reigning in life through Jesus Christ as well.

2. Thank You Father that Jesus came to bind up the broken-hearted, to proclaim freedom for the captives and release from darkness for the prisoners, to proclaim the year of the Lord's favor, to comfort all who mourn, to provide for those who grieve in Zion, to bestow on them a crown of beauty instead of ashes, the oil of gladness instead of mourning and a garment of praise instead of a spirit of despair. I declare over myself and my family that we are set free, healed, comforted, delivered from darkness and filled with joy and praise for the one and only true God (see Isaiah 61:1-3).

3. Thank You Father, in Jesus' Name, for giving **us** (your name and other people's names that you are praying for) the spirit of wisdom and revelation so that we may know You better. Thank You for enlightening the eyes of our hearts so that we may know the hope to which You have called us, the riches of Your glorious inheritance in the saints and Your incomparably great power for us who believe (see Ephesians 1:17-19).

4. Thank You Father, in Jesus' Name, for strengthening **us** (names) out of Your glorious riches of grace with power through Your Spirit in our inner being so that Christ may dwell in our hearts through faith. Thank You for rooting and grounding us in Your love and helping us to grasp how wide and long and high and deep is the love of Christ for us personally and to know this love by personal experiences with You. Thank You that we are filled with Your love and with the fullness of God Himself. Thank You Lord that You do exceedingly, abundantly, above and beyond all that we could ever ask, imagine or think according to Your great power that is at work within us for Your glory, in Jesus' Name (see Ephesians 3:14-21).

5. Thank You Father for filling **us** (names) with the knowledge of Your will through all spiritual wisdom and understanding, in Jesus' Name (see Colossians 1:9).

These are prayers that Paul prayed for the Ephesian and Colossian Churches.

6. Thank You Lord that You are **our** Shepherd. We shall not be in want. You make us lie down in green pastures. You lead us beside quiet waters. You restore our soul. You guide us in paths of righteousness for Your name's sake. Even though we walk through the valley of the shadow of death, we will fear no evil for You are with us, Your rod and Your staff comfort us. You prepare a table before us in the presence of our enemies. You anoint our head with oil, our cup overflows. Surely goodness and love shall follow us all the days of our lives and we will dwell in the house of the Lord forever, in Jesus' Name (see Psalm 23).

7. Psalm 91 is another powerful psalm that can be turned into a prayer.

If you can memorize these scriptures, you can pray them wherever you are.

There are so many scriptures that you can turn into a prayer that is perfect for your situation or someone else's situation. As you read the Word, ask the Holy Spirit to show you scriptures that you can turn into a prayer.

Did you notice that I began each prayer thanking God for His promises that I was about to pray? By doing this, I am declaring that it is already mine. When you pray, thank Him for the answer and receive it as Jesus has already provided everything you need in His redemptive work on the cross. Don't pray the problem. Pray the answer. Speak life over yourself and your loved ones. When Jesus said just before He died "It is finished" He was saying I have already provided for you everything you need. Now receive it. It's yours.

When we pray and declare God's Word we are releasing the supernatural power of God into the heavenlies.

The storm can be raging all around us but we can have peace in the middle of the storm and walk on water (our sorrows, etc.) when we keep our eyes on Jesus, who is our Victory.

Let Jesus' Joy Rise Up In You

*J*esus' joy is part of your inheritance. So let's look at and consider some scriptures on joy. By meditating on these scriptures, joy will begin to rise up in your heart and it will break out of you if you let it.

There are some prophetic acts that I will ask you to do throughout this section of the Book. Please do them as it will make a huge difference in your life and bring a great reward.

There are also many prayers and declarations throughout this Chapter. As you pray and declare God's Word, you are releasing angelic beings to minister on your behalf.

> *"Fire came out from the presence of the Lord and consumed the burnt offering and the fat portions on the altar. And when all the people saw it, they shouted for **joy** and fell face down" (Leviticus 9:24, emphasis added).*

The people of old were offering a sacrifice to God and God accepted their sacrifice with fire. This showed the people that God was there in their midst. When the people saw the **presence of God**, they shouted for joy. **In the presence of the Lord is fullness of joy.**

> *"Celebrate the Feast of Tabernacles for seven days after you have gathered the produce of your threshing*

*floor and your winepress. Be **joyful** at your Feast*
– you, your sons & daughters, your menservants
and maidservants and the Levites, the aliens, the
fatherless and the widows who live in your towns.
For seven days celebrate the Feast to the Lord your
God at the place the Lord will choose. For the Lord
your God will bless you in all your harvest and in all
*the work of your hands, and your **joy** will be complete"*
(Deuteronomy 16:13-15, emphasis added).

God wants you to be joyful and to celebrate Him and He will bless you in all your harvest and in all the work of your hands and your joy will be complete. **This is the will of God for you.**

Prayer: Father, in Jesus' Name, by Your grace enable me to obey Your Word to be joyful and to celebrate You. As I read and meditate on Your Word, destroy the yokes of bondage in my life so that I may worship thee and walk in joy. Help me to apply Your Word to my everyday living.

You can make a choice in your heart right now to celebrate Jesus. Throughout this day, you can choose to celebrate Jesus. You can say "I choose to celebrate you Lord Jesus" over and over throughout this day. Ask God to put a song of celebration in your heart. As you sing this song over and over, God will lift you up.

"These are the numbers of the men armed for battle
who came to David at Hebron to turn Saul's kingdom
over to him, as the Lord had said. All these were
fighting men who volunteered to serve in the ranks.
They came to Hebron fully determined to make David
king over all Israel. All the rest of the Israelites were
*also of **one mind** to make David king. There were*
plentiful supplies of flour, fig cakes, raisin cakes,
*wine, oil, cattle and sheep, for there was **joy** in Israel"*
(1 Chronicles 12:23, 38, 40b, emphasis added).

It is God's desire that His people walk in unity and be of one mind, having the mind of Christ. It was God's Will to make David King over all Israel. As God's people understood the mind/will of God and joined together in unity to bring this about, it brought great joy to them.

Is there disunity in your life that is robbing you of joy? When you surrender your will, by the grace of God, to His Will, and come into unity in the Spirit with those around you, you too will have very great joy. Ask God to show you how you can come into unity with your spouse and others without compromising your faith in God.

> *"They found written in the Law, which the Lord had commanded through Moses, that the Israelites were to live in booths during the feast of the seventh month. The whole company that had returned from exile built booths and lived in them. From the days of Joshua son of Nun until that day, the Israelites had not celebrated it like this. And their **joy** was very great"* (Nehemiah 8:14, 17, emphasis added).

The whole company, which represents unity, walked in obedience to God and there was very great joy. They had just returned from living in exile back to their homeland and back into an intimate relationship with God.

By the grace of God, you can walk in unity and in the Will of God for your life without compromising your faith in God. By the grace of God, you too will have very great joy.

Prayer: Father, in Jesus' Name, help me to walk in unity without compromising my faith in You and draw me close to You so that I may have great joy. Please show me Your Will for my life.

> *"Glory in his holy name; let the hearts of those who seek the Lord **rejoice"** (1 Chronicles 16:10, emphasis added).*

We are to seek God with rejoicing. Is your heart seeking/desiring God? If not, ask God for His grace to seek Him. Don't condemn yourself. Rather pray and trust God to give you a desire to seek Him. There have been short times in my Christian walk when I was so full of sorrow and grief that I had lost my desire to spend time with God.

During those times, I prayed and trusted Him to draw me into His Presence and into His Word and He did. Pray and then let Him do it. He desires your presence and He will draw you.

> *"Splendor and majesty are before him;* **strength** *and* **joy** *in his dwelling place" (1 Chronicles 16:27, emphasis added).*

When we abide or dwell in the presence of the Lord, we are strengthened in the most holy faith and we are filled with joy.

Prayer: Father, help me to abide in Your presence, strengthen me in the most holy faith and fill me with Your joy. Please give me a desire to know You better through Your Word, in Jesus' Name.

> *"The next day they made sacrifices to the Lord and presented burnt offerings to him: a thousand bulls, a thousand rams and a thousand male lambs, together with their drink offerings and other sacrifices in abundance for all Israel. They ate and drank with great* **joy** *in the presence of the Lord that day" (1 Chronicles 29:21-22a, emphasis added).*

The Israelites offered up animal sacrifices, but you can offer up to God sacrifices of joy. When you don't feel joyful, you can decide to offer up to God a sacrifice of joy. That is why it is called a sacrifice. Just laugh out loud or look up to heaven and smile. As you do this and continue to do it, you will experience great joy in your life. Laughing and smiling when you don't feel like it, is a prophetic act of faith and a sacrifice to God. I have done this many times. In the midst of my sorrow, I would purposely laugh out loud. This prophetic laugh releases the power of God in your life.

Prophetic Act: Go ahead and laugh out loud right now.

> *"For seven days they celebrated with* **joy** *the Feast of Unleavened Bread, because the Lord had filled them with joy by changing the attitude of the king of Assyria,*

so that he assisted them in the work on the house of God, the God of Israel" (Ezra 6:22, emphasis added).

I noticed here that "Unleavened Bread" is capitalized. This is a shadow or type of the Lord Jesus Christ who is the Bread of Life. Unleavened Bread means there is no yeast in the Bread. Jesus told the people to guard themselves from the yeast of the Pharisees and Sadducees referring to their teaching which was false. In 1 Corinthians 5:6 it says to get rid of the old yeast, the yeast of malice and wickedness and to take the bread without yeast, the bread of sincerity and truth. Jesus represents the Bread without yeast. Jesus represents purity, truth and life. As we eat of this Bread which is the Word of God, it sustains us, nourishes us, strengthens us and brings joy into our lives.

Prayer: Thank You Father that Jesus is the Bread of Life. Help me to eat this Bread which is the Word of God so that I will be nourished and strengthened in the most holy faith. Help me to get the Word in my heart and coming out of my mouth so that I will experience Your joy in my life, in Jesus' Name.

*"Nehemiah said "Go and enjoy choice food and sweet drinks, and send some to those who have nothing prepared. This day is sacred to our Lord. Do not grieve, for the **joy** of the Lord is your strength" (Nehemiah 8:10, emphasis added).*

God does not want you to grieve (be sorrowful) because grieving will rob you of strength and enjoyment of life. Joy brings you strength. God wants you to enjoy your life. Joy is a spiritual weapon and gives you strength against sorrow, sadness, depression, etc. Have you ever thought of joy being a spiritual weapon before?

Prayer: Father, in Jesus' Name, I thank You for setting me free from grief and sorrow, sadness and depression and every negative emotion so that I can walk and live in Your joy. Thank You for setting me free from everything that would overwhelm me and discourage me. Thank You Jesus that You took these negative emotions upon Yourself on the cross for me personally. I lay them at the foot of Your cross. They have no power over me. These negative emotions have been crucified with Christ and they can no longer live in me. I choose to receive Your joy and the victory over them that You accomplished for me personally on the cross. I receive Your healing to my heart. I receive the freedom that You accomplished for me in Your redemptive work. This day I choose life, the Bread of Life, the God kind of life, a life filled with joy, peace and righteousness in the Holy Spirit. Thank You Jesus that You redeemed me from the curse of the law by becoming a curse for me. The curse over my emotions is destroyed and the blessings of God are flowing. My emotions are now blessed. Therefore, I can declare "I have blessed emotions". Hallelujah!!!

> *"At the dedication of the wall of Jerusalem, the Levites were sought out from where they lived and were brought to Jerusalem to celebrate joyfully the dedication with songs of thanksgiving and with the music of cymbals, harps and lyres. And on that day they offered great sacrifices, rejoicing because God had given them great joy. The women and children also rejoiced. The sound of rejoicing in Jerusalem could be heard far away"* (Nehemiah 12:27, 43, emphasis added).

When you read between the verses 27 and 43, you will see a well organized mass of people with thankful hearts singing, playing instruments, and making a joyful noise unto the Lord that could be heard far away. God had given them a great victory. They had finished rebuilding the wall of Jerusalem and they were dedicating it to God. They had experienced a lot of opposition while building the wall and it was now complete.

This was a celebration that was unified. It was not a bunch of people doing their own thing. They were coming joyfully, with thankful hearts, before the Lord as one Body united together submitting to their leadership and ultimately to the Lord.

In the Book of Esther, Naman hated Morcedai, who was a Jewish man, and wanted to kill him as well as all of the Jews in all the provinces. The King found out about this plot by Naman through Queen Esther and had Naman and his family killed.

In this next scripture reference Morcedai was honored by the King and the Jewish people were given the authority to fight back against their attackers and God gave them a great victory.

> *"Morcedai left the king's presence wearing royal garments of blue and white, a large crown of gold and a purple robe of fine linen. And the city of Susa held a joyous celebration. For the Jews, it was a time of happiness and joy, gladness and honor. In every province and in every city, wherever the edict of the king went, there was joy and gladness among the Jews, with feasting and celebrating. And many people of other nationalities became Jews because fear of the Jews had seized them" (Esther 8:15, 17).*

Victories and answers to prayer brings joy, celebration, happiness, gladness & honor. Think about the times that God answered your prayers and celebrate this victory. Come before Him with a thankful and grateful heart as you remember all the times that the Lord has answered your prayers. Can you do that now? Take a few minutes and remember what the Lord has done for you personally and thank Him for it. This will bring encouragement and joy to you.

When people see God answering our prayers and bringing us great victories and see us rejoicing and celebrating, they will want what we have and get saved.

Prior to this victory, Queen Esther had to put **her faith into action**. Her actions could have caused her to lose her life. The Jewish community fasted and prayed and God granted Queen Esther and her people favor with the King. I would encourage you to read the Book of Esther so that you too will put your faith into action. If Esther would not have put her faith into action, she and all her people would have perished.

Through this victory for the Jews, other nationalities saw that the Jews were highly favored by God and they were afraid of the Jews. Instead of fighting the Jews, many decided to join them because they realized God was on their side. The Jews were God's chosen people. Other people with different nationalities could unite themselves with the Jewish people and be part of God's chosen people. Now that Jesus has died on the cross for us and has risen from the dead, when we choose Jesus as our personal Savior and Lord, we become one of God's chosen people. Jesus, being God in the flesh, died for all mankind so that all who believe in Him will not perish but have eternal life.

> *"This happened on the thirteenth day of the month of Adar, and on the fourteenth they rested and made it a day of feasting and **joy**" (Esther 9:17, emphasis added).*

God had given the Jews a great victory and the Jews thanked God by celebrating this victory with thanksgiving and joy. They put aside other things on their agenda and decided to honor God with a celebration. We can decide to celebrate Jesus and our victories right here and now **by faith**. We can begin to thank Jesus for the victory right now even though we have not yet seen it. God loves it when we set time aside to fellowship with Him, to thank Him and enjoy Him in our lives.

Prayer: **By faith** I thank You Father, in Jesus' Name, for the victory over depression, sorrow, sadness, grief and every like thing. I receive it by faith. I thank You for it and I rejoice in my victory.

> *"Morcedai recorded these events and he sent letters to all the Jews throughout the provinces of King Xerxes, near and far, to have them celebrate annually the 14th & 15th days of the month of Adar as the time when the Jews got relief from their enemies and as the month when **their sorrow was turned into joy** and their mourning into a day of celebration. He wrote them to observe the days as days of feasting and joy and giving presents of food to one another and gifts to the poor" (Esther 9:20-22, emphasis added).*

The Jewish people had humbled themselves before the Lord in prayer and fasting and God heard and brought about a great victory which resulted in a celebration of joy. God turned their sorrow into joy and their mourning into a day of celebration.

Morcedai had the Jews celebrate this feast annually so that they would **remember** what the Lord did for them and pass it on to future generations.

Prayer: Father, in Jesus' Name, empower me by Your Spirit to honor You by purposing in my heart to be joyful. Empower me to put my faith into action. Empower me to walk by faith and not by sight. Empower me to put on joy even when I don't feel like doing it. Empower me to praise and worship You even when I am feeling down. Please put me in remembrance of all the things in my life that I can be thankful for.

You've just asked God to empower you by His Spirit. Now put your faith into action. Begin to praise and worship Him. Begin to thank Him for the things you can be thankful for. Begin to thank Him for who He is. Begin to thank Him for He is good and He is faithful. Begin to put your focus on Him, get your focus off of yourself and allow Him to bring you into His Presence.

> *"He prays to God and finds favour with him, he sees God's face and shouts for joy, he is restored by God to his righteous state" (Job 33:26, emphasis added).*

When we behold God in the secret place, there is joy. It can cause us to quietly soak in His Presence or shout for joy on the roof tops.

Prophetic Act: Go ahead and shout unto God and praise His holy Name. Hallelujah Jesus!!!!!!! Go ahead and shout it out loud. Hallelujah Jesus!!!!!!! You may not feel like it, but don't be led by your feelings. Put your faith into action and shout out the Name of Jesus!!!!!!!

You may not realize it but power is released from heaven when you do this.

> *"You have filled my heart with greater joy than when their grain and new wine abound. I will lie down and sleep in peace, for you alone, O Lord, make me dwell in safety" (Psalm 4:7-8, emphasis added).*

Joy satisfies the soul and brings us a rest from anxiety and worry causing us to sleep peacefully.

When God moves in our lives, it brings a greater joy than the bounty of the wicked. There is no comparison.

Prayer: Father, in Jesus' Name, I lay at the cross all anxiety, worry, sorrow and fear and I receive Your joy, rest and peaceful sleep.

> *"But let all who take refuge in you be glad; let them ever sing for joy. Spread your protection over them, that those who love your name may rejoice in you. For surely, O Lord, you bless the righteous; you surround them with your favor as with a shield" (Psalm 5:11-12, emphasis added).*

It is a sure thing that God blesses all those who receive Him as their Savior and Lord and who take refuge in Him. He surrounds us on every side with His favor. He is our shield of favor. God blesses us with joyful hearts and gives us His favor and protection. This is something to sing about. This is something to shout about.

Prayer: Father, in Jesus' Name, thank You that You are my refuge, that I am blessed with a joyful heart and that I have favor with You and man. Thank You for Your protection and Your unmerited favor that surrounds me and my family like a shield. Thank You Father, in Jesus' Name, that we are highly favored, greatly blessed and deeply loved.

Speak forth God's promises regularly and these promises will manifest in your life.

> *"You have made known to me the path of life; you will fill me with joy in your presence, with eternal pleasures at your right hand" (Psalm 16:11, emphasis added).*

God reveals to us the path that leads to life and joy. Jesus is the way (path), the truth and the life. What greater joy is there than to know that we can enjoy God's Presence right now and for all eternity. If you have never received Jesus as your personal Savior and Lord and you want a personal relationship with Jesus, you can say the following prayer, and if you mean it with your whole heart, you will be saved.

Prayer: Father, in Jesus' Name, please forgive me for my sins and cleanse me from all unrighteousness. Jesus I believe You died on the cross for me and rose from the dead so that I could have a personal relationship/friendship with You. I receive You into my life as my personal Savior and Lord. You took all my sins and You gave me Your righteousness. I receive forgiveness for my sins. I receive Your grace and Your gift of righteousness to reign in life. Please help me, by the power of Your Holy Spirit, to walk in Your grace and Your righteousness all the days of my life and help me to renew my mind with Your Word. I am now right with You. Thank You Jesus for saving me and filling me with Your joy.

> *"The precepts of the Lord are right, giving **joy** to the heart" (Psalm 19:8, emphasis added).*

Precepts refer to God's Word. As you put God's Word into your heart and apply it to your life, you will have joy. This is God's promise to you. He says that His Word will give joy to your heart.

> *"We will shout for **joy** when you are victorious and will lift up our banners in the name of our God. May the Lord grant all your requests" (Psalm 20:5, emphasis added).*

As we pray for ourselves and others and we see God meet needs and move in our lives, we will shout for joy. Victories bring joy (exuberant joy) to us and praise to God.

You have been praying prayers throughout this book. As you experience the results of these prayers, shout your praises to God with a voice of triumph.

> *"O Lord, the king rejoices in your strength. How great is his **joy** in the victories you give! You have granted him the desire of his heart and have not withheld the requests of his lips. You welcomed him with rich blessings and placed a crown of pure gold on his head. Surely you have granted him eternal blessings and made him glad with the **joy** of your presence" (Psalm 21:1-3, 6, emphasis added).*

When God displays His mighty power and gives us the desire of our heart that is in accordance with His Will, great joy is released in us. God gives us the victory. He makes us victorious. Victory brings great joy. There is fullness of joy in the Presence of the Lord.

Prayer: Thank You Father, in Jesus' Name, that I am victorious in Christ. You have given me the victory. I already have it by faith, whether I feel it or not, whether I see it or not. **By faith** I declare that I have the victory over sorrow, sadness, grief, depression and everything that would try to rob me of joy.

As we continue to thank God for the victory, we will see and experience the manifestation of what we are believing Him for. Always remember that when we pray, we pray from a place of victory and not from a place of defeat. Jesus has already fought and won the battle for us. Our fight is the good fight of faith. This means that our fight is to continue to believe in Jesus and in His finished works on the cross. It means that our fight is to continue to believe that Jesus has won the battle on our behalf. That is why it is called a good fight. It is a good fight because we win if we do not give up.

> *"For in the day of trouble he will keep me safe in his dwelling; he will hide me in the shelter of his tabernacle and set me high upon a rock. Then my head will be exalted above the enemies who surround me; at his tabernacle will I sacrifice with shouts of joy; I will sing and make music to the Lord" (Psalm 27:5-6, emphasis added).*

The Psalmist is talking about being in the presence of the Lord in the day of trouble. Are you in trouble? If so, ask God to hide you in the shelter of His Presence and then know that you are safe in His dwelling (tabernacle), that He sets you high upon a rock and that He exalts you above your enemies.

Prayer: Father, please hide me in the shelter of Your Presence, in Jesus' Name. Thank You Jesus that you are my hiding place.

> *"Praise be to the Lord, for he has heard my cry for mercy. The Lord is my strength and my shield; my*

heart trusts in him, and I am helped. My heart leaps
for joy and I will give thanks to him in song" (Psalm
28:6-7, emphasis added).

I can leap for joy because I know my God is faithful to help me
and protect me.

Prophetic Act: Go ahead and leap for joy. This is a prophetic act
of faith. Go ahead, get out of your chair and jump for joy.

Something good is released in the heavenlies when you, by faith,
do these prophetic acts.

"You turned my wailing into dancing; you removed
my sackcloth and clothed me with joy; that my heart
may sing to you and not be silent. O Lord my God,
I will give you thanks forever" (Psalm 30:11-12,
emphasis added).

Prayer: Father, in Jesus' Name, thank You that Jesus has already
delivered me from all sorrow, sadness, mourning, depression, discouragement, and all like things. Thank You that Jesus has already
removed these things from me. He has already set me free from them
according to Isaiah 61:1-3. I receive the freedom that Jesus died to
give me by faith. I am filled with Your joy now and You have set my
feet to dancing for You are the One and only true God.

"Sing joyfully to the Lord, you righteous; it is fitting
for the upright to praise him. Praise the Lord with
the harp; make music to him on the ten-stringed lyre.
Sing to him a new song; play skillfully and shout for
joy" (Psalm 33:1-3, emphasis added).

God deserves our praise and shouts of joy. He deserves our worship. He deserves for us to use our talents and gifts to honor Him.
God does not need our praise and worship but He absolutely delights
when we do it. When we praise and worship God and shout for joy,
we will benefit from it.

Start shouting your praise to the King of glory now.

Declarations: Thank You Jesus that You are my Healer. You are my Savior. You are my Deliverer. You are my Life. You are my Strength. I praise Your Holy Name for You are worthy to be praised. You are the Lifter of my head and the Lover of my soul. You are my God and I am Your child. I belong to You. You are my everything. You love me unconditionally. I love You, Jesus. I honor You. Thank You for being in my life. Thank You that I am in the palm of Your hand and that You care for me.

This is something to shout about!!! Hallelujah Jesus!!! Thank You Jesus that you are my ever present help in times of trouble!!! I am victorious in You, Jesus!!!

As you continue to make these declarations, the negative emotions you are experiencing will begin to leave you and joy will begin to arise within your soul.

> *"May those who delight in my vindication* **shout for joy** *and gladness; may they always say, "The Lord be exalted, who delights in the well being of his servant"* *(Psalm 35:27, emphasis added).*

God delights in our well being. God is for us, not against us. He wants us whole in every area of our lives. It is His desire to see us joyful even when we are going through rough times. It shows Him that we are trusting Him, that we are looking to Him, that we have our eyes focused on Him and not on the circumstances.

Prayer: Father, in Jesus' Name, help me to focus on You and not on my circumstances. Help me to keep looking at Jesus and to walk on my circumstances just like Peter did when he got out of the boat. I choose to walk on all the negative emotions in my life and I choose to allow the joy of the Lord to come forth and break out of me.

> *"These things I remember as I pour out my soul how I used to go with the multitude, leading the procession to the house of God, with shouts of* **joy** *and thanksgiving among the festive throng"* *(Psalm 42:4, emphasis added).*

When you are with other Christians who are festively praising and worshipping God, this will help you to be lifted up out of despair and sorrow, if you will let it. Your thoughts will be turned to the Lord and off of your circumstances. God wants you to meet together with other believers who praise and worship God jubilantly. This is for your benefit. You are lifted up out of that despair when you praise and worship God with other believers. You honor God when you praise and worship Him.

Get together with other believers. If you are not in a Church, ask God to lead you to the right Church for you so that you can have fellowship with other believers and experience corporate worship. It is powerful when believers corporately worship God.

> *"Send forth your light and your truth, let them guide me; let them bring me to your holy mountain, to the place where you dwell. Then will I go to the altar of God, to God my **joy** and my delight. I will praise you with the harp, O God, my God" (Psalm 43:3-4, emphasis added).*

God's Word sheds light into my situation. Through His Word, He guides me into all truth and into the fullness of joy. God's Word brings me direction and joy.

A good full Gospel Bible believing Church that is led by the Holy Spirit is an instrument used by God to teach us the Word of God. It is God's Will for us to be connected with other members of the Body of Christ on a regular basis so that we will be built up, encouraged in the most holy faith and strengthened by God Himself.

Prayer: Father, shine Your light upon me and my family that we may be set free by the truth and experience You intimately and personally in our everyday life, that we may know Your direction and that we may have Your joy. Lead us to the Church where we will have fellowship with other believers and hear Your Word so that we may grow, be encouraged, built up and strengthened in the most holy faith, in Jesus' Name.

*"Your throne, O God, will last for ever and ever; a scepter of justice will be the scepter of your kingdom, you love righteousness and hate wickedness; therefore God, your God, has set you above your companions by anointing you with the oil of **joy**" (Psalm 45:6, emphasis added).*

God, the Father, is talking to God, His Son, in this scripture.

Jesus was anointed with the oil of joy. As a child of God, you are in Christ and all that belongs to Jesus is yours. Therefore, in Christ, you are anointed with the oil of joy as well, for Jesus' joy resides in you. Think about this. You are anointed with the oil of joy because Jesus resides in you. Go ahead and declare it out loud.

Declaration: "I am anointed with the oil of joy."

Say it a few times.

*"All glorious is the princess within her chamber; her gown is interwoven with **gold**. In embroidered garments she is led to the **king**; her **virgin** companions follow her and are brought to you. They are led in with **joy and gladness**; they enter the palace of the king" (Psalm 45:13-15, emphasis added).*

Gold represents royalty. We are the King's kids. We are royalty because we are God's children.

Virgin represents purity and holiness. We are made pure when we receive the redemptive work of Christ on the cross.

The King represents Jesus. We are to come before the Lord Jesus with joy, gladness and purity of heart and as the King's kids (His children). Think about a King's kid and the benefits that kid has just by simply being born into a royal family. When we are born into the family of God, think of the benefits we have by simply being born again into God's family. When we repent of our sins and receive Jesus into our hearts as our personal Savior and make Him the Lord of our lives, we are born again (born into the family of God) and He daily loads us with His benefits.

Declarations: "I am royalty. I am the King's kid. I belong to Jesus. He has made me righteous by giving me His righteousness. I am right with Him. Because I am His child, I receive all the benefits that have been made available to me. I receive my full inheritance in Christ Jesus by faith."

> *"Clap your hands, all you nations; shout to God with cries of joy. How awesome is the Lord most high, the great King over all the earth!" (Psalm 47:1-2, emphasis added)*

When we get a revelation of how awesome God is, we will **clap our hands** and **shout to God** with tears of joy. We will **jump exuberantly** and not care about being dignified. We won't care about what others think because we will be so enamored with Jesus.

Prophetic Act: Start clapping your hands and shouting to God. Get up and jump exuberantly before Him.

Prayer: Father, give me a revelation of how awesome You, Jesus and Holy Spirit are. Help me to see You the way You really are. Help me to see You through spiritual eyes and not the eyes of my flesh. Also, help me to see myself and others through Your eyes of love and not the eyes of my flesh. Help me to value myself and others in the same way that Jesus values me. Help me to know Your love for me personally and by experience, in Jesus' Name.

> *"God has ascended amid shouts of joy, the Lord amid the sounding of trumpets. Sing praises to God, sing praises; sing praises to our King, sing praises. For God is the King of all the earth; sing to him a psalm of praise. God reigns over the nations; God is seated on his holy throne" (Psalm 47:5-8, emphasis added).*

When we shout for joy to Jesus and continue to do so, He is exalted and lifted up in our hearts. At the same time we lift Him up in our hearts, He comes upon us from above with His glory and the atmosphere around us is charged with His manifested Presence. The Bible talks about the glory cloud settling upon us. One reference is

Exodus 24:15. "When Moses went up on the mountain, the cloud covered it, and the glory of the Lord settled on Mount Sinai."

So when we shout for joy to Jesus and continue to do so, He rises up within us and His glory settles upon us. We are filled with His Presence inwardly and surrounded by His Presence outwardly.

Prayer: Father, in Jesus' Name, help me to praise You and to shout for joy so that I may experience Your Presence inside and outside of me.

> *"Great is the Lord and most worthy of praise, in the city of our God, his holy mountain. It is beautiful in its loftiness, the joy of the whole earth" (Psalm 48:1-2a, emphasis added).*

The place where God dwells is the joy of the whole earth because He dwells there. It is not the place but God Himself that brings joy. Just being in the atmosphere where God is present brings us joy. It is His Presence that fills us with His joy. In God's Presence, the whole earth can find joy.

One of the names of God is "Jehovah Shammah" which means "My Abiding Presence".

Prayer: Father, in Jesus' Name, thank You that You are Jehovah Shammah, my Abiding Presence. Thank You that You never leave me nor forsake me. Thank You for Your Abiding Presence in my life.

> *"Restore to me the joy of your salvation and grant me a willing spirit to sustain me" (Psalm 51:12, emphasis added).*

The Psalmist is asking God two things here. He had lost the joy of salvation and was asking God to restore joy to him. He also asked God to help him live in that joy. Since salvation is eternal the Psalmist wanted eternal joy. He wanted joy that would not be temporal but everlasting joy.

Prayer: Father, in Jesus' Name, I ask that You would help me to live in eternal joy, Your joy that will sustain me from day to day.

"Those living far away fear your wonders; where morning dawns and evening fades, you call forth songs of joy" (Psalm 65:8, emphasis added).

The unsaved who are living far from God will walk in fear, but God brings forth songs of joy to those who know Him and walk close with Him, day by day. When we seek God, songs of joy will come forth from within us.

Prayer: Father, in Jesus' Name, put a song of deliverance in my heart and help me to sing it until the victory comes.

"Shout with joy to God, all the earth! Sing the glory of his name; make the praise glorious" (Psalm 66:1, emphasis added).

Sing and glorify the Name of Jesus, the Name that is above all names. At the Name of Jesus every knee shall bow and every tongue confess that Jesus Christ is Lord to the glory of God the Father. The enemy cringes at the Name of Jesus and must submit to His Name.

Prophetic Act: Shout to God right now. Hallelujah Jesus!!!!! I praise you Lord Jesus!!!!! Raise your hands to heaven, close your eyes and shout it again with all your might.

Continue to praise Him and thank Him for dying on the cross for you and whatever else you want to thank and praise Him for.

"But may the righteous be glad and rejoice before God; may they be happy and joyful. Sing to God, sing praise to his name, extol him who rides on the clouds – his name is the Lord – and rejoice before him. He leads forth the prisoners with singing" (Psalm 68:3, 4, 6b, emphasis added).

When you are joyful before the Lord, bondages are broken off of you and you are set free from captivity. You walk out of your prison cell into freedom and victory. God wants you to be joyful. This is His Will for your life. Even if you don't feel like praising God, do it anyway. This is a sacrifice of praise offered up to God who is worthy to be praised.

Prayer: Father, in Jesus' Name, help me to praise You even when I don't feel like it.

> *"Sing for joy to God our strength; shout aloud to the*
> *God of Jacob" (Psalm 81:1, emphasis added).*

When I sing and shout to God, His power is released into the atmosphere around and about me and it affects me positively. Joy will bring strength to me in every area of my life.

> *"Bring joy to your servant, for to you, O Lord, I lift up*
> *my soul" (Psalm 86:4, emphasis added).*

Joy comes from God. Joy lives in us because Jesus lives in us and He is full of joy. Joy is part of my inheritance in Christ Jesus. Joy belongs to me.

Prayer: Father, in Jesus' Name, thank You for giving me joy as my inheritance. I receive it now.

> *"Satisfy us in the morning with your unfailing love,*
> *that we may sing for joy and be glad all our days"*
> *(Psalm 90:14, emphasis added).*

When we know how much God loves us, we will sing for joy.

Prayer: Father, pour Your love into my heart so that I may know You, Jesus and Holy Spirit personally, intimately and by experience. Satisfy me each morning with Your unfailing love. Your Word says that Your mercies are new every morning. Please remind me to receive Your mercies that are new every morning that I need for that day, in Jesus' Name.

> *"For you make me glad by your deeds, O Lord; I sing*
> *for joy at the works of your hands. How great are your*
> *works, O Lord, how profound your thoughts!" (Psalm*
> *92:4-5, emphasis added)*

Just looking around us and seeing God's creation, His power displayed and answers to our prayers, makes us glad and joyful. What do you think when you see a rainbow, a beautiful sunset, freshly fallen snow or ice hanging on trees and bushes? What do you think when God gives you a revelation or some wisdom when you need it? What do you think when God does something special for you? I think about how awesome God is and about how much He loves and cares for me. These things make me glad and they make me want to praise Him even more.

> *"When anxiety was great within me, your consolation brought joy to my soul" (Psalm 94:19, emphasis added).*

There is no comfort like the comfort of the Lord. It turns anxiety into peace, tears into laughter, and sorrow into joy.

Prayer: Father, in Jesus' Name, thank You for comforting me with the comfort only You can give. Thank You for turning my anxiety into peace, my tears into laughter and my sorrow into joy.

> *"Come, let us sing for joy to the Lord; let us shout aloud to the Rock of our salvation. Let us come before him with thanksgiving and extol him with music and song. For the Lord is the great God, the great King above all gods. In his hand are the depths of the earth and the mountain peaks belong to him. The sea is his, for he made it, and his hands formed the dry ground. Come, let us bow down in worship, let us kneel before the Lord our maker; for he is our God and we are the people of his pasture, the flock under his care" (Psalm 95:1-7, emphasis added).*

When I think about the majesty of God and all that He has made, it makes me want to shout and dance and sing and worship before Him. When I witness the miracle of a baby coming forth from a mother's womb, a puppy, kitten, calf, pony, etc. being born, when I look at a tiny insect that looks like a black speck but it is crawling and I know that God even has food for this little speck of a creature, I can stand in awe of my God. When I realize that God is so big that He holds the whole earth in the palm of His hand, I can rest assured that He is able to take care of me.

> *"Let the heavens rejoice, let the earth be glad, let the sea resound and all that is in it; let the fields be jubilant and everything in them. Then all the trees of the forest will sing for joy"* (Psalm 96:11-12, emphasis added).

When we see the trees moving with the wind in every direction, they are clapping their hands to God and giving Him praise. When we see waves pounding up on its shores, they are bringing forth praise to God. When we see the flowers and plants of the fields sprouting and blooming, they are singing for joy to God.

What an awesome God we serve who surrounds us with a continual revelation of His power and love for us even in difficult times. Praise comes forth from all His creation.

Prayer: Father, in Jesus' Name, help me to understand Your ways and to know You more and more each and every day and to follow You and only You. Help me to keep my focus on You. Thank You for delivering me out of darkness and bringing me into Your glorious light to dwell with You. Father, in Jesus' Name, I know that in this world I will have trouble, but You have made a way for me to be an overcomer. Your Word says that I am more than a conqueror in Christ Jesus. Draw me close to You and help me to remain in the palm of Your hand so that I may walk in victory. Help me to have peace and joy even in the middle of the storms of life. Guide my footsteps each and every day so that I may walk in Your Will for my life.

> *"Light is shed upon the righteous and joy upon the upright in heart. Rejoice in the Lord, you who are righteous and praise his holy name"* (Psalm 97:11-12, emphasis added).

Praise and Declarations: Hallelujah Jesus!!!! I rejoice in You and I praise Your holy Name. You are holy and there is none like You, O

Lord. You are my refuge and my fortress. You are my stronghold and it is in You I put my trust.

> *"**Shout** for joy to the Lord, all the earth; **burst** into jubilant song with music; **make music** to the Lord with the harp and the sound of singing, with trumpets and the blast of the ram's horn – **shout** for joy before the Lord the King. Let the sea resound and everything in it, the world and all who live in it. Let the rivers **clap** their hands; let the mountains **sing** together for joy" (Psalm 98:4-8, emphasis added).*

This gives us a picture of all of creation shouting and making a joyful loud noise to God.

The scripture says to "burst" into "jubilant" song. Take a moment and picture people doing this. It is not a passive sight. People will stand up and do the "wave" in a stadium watching a hockey game or a football game. They are doing this simply for men playing a sport. What about doing something like this for the God of all creation who died and gave His life for you and who loves you unconditionally.

Prophetic Act: Go ahead and do the wave for Jesus. Stand up and do the wave for the King of glory for He alone is worthy of all praise.

> *"**Shout** for joy to the Lord all the earth. **Worship** the Lord with gladness; come before him with **joyful songs**. Enter his gates with **thanksgiving** and his courts with praise; **give thanks** to him and **praise his name**" (Psalm 100: 1, 2, 4, emphasis added).*

These verses are telling us what to do. Shout for joy, worship with gladness, sing joyfully, be thankful, give thanks, and praise His name. If you are down, this will take a concerted effort on your behalf but the results will be rewarding.

Praise and Declarations: Hallelujah Jesus!!!!! You are the King of kings and the Lord of lords. You are Almighty God. You are full of grace and most worthy to be praised. I love You Jesus and I put my faith, hope and trust in You alone. You are Jehovah Rophe, my Healer. You are

Jehovah Shammah, My Abiding Presence. You are Adonai, my Master. You are Jehovah Nissi, my Banner, my Covering and my Protection. You are Jehovah Jireh, my Provider. You are Jehovah Shalom, my Peace.

> *"He brought out his people with rejoicing, his chosen ones with shouts of joy" (Psalm 105:43, emphasis added).*

What did he bring His people out from? Slavery, bondage, poverty, mistreatment, sorrow, depression, etc. These things come from the enemy of our souls. The Bible says that the thief comes to rob, steal, kill and destroy but Jesus came to give us life and give it to us abundantly (see John 10:10).

Shouts of joy is a powerful spiritual force. The enemy cringes when we shout with joy to God.

Prophetic Act: Hallelujah Jesus!!!!!

When you do this, you are fighting the sorrow and grief in your heart and it begins to leave you. The more you put this into practice in your life, the quicker the victory will come.

> *"Shouts of joy and victory resound in the tents of the righteous: The Lord's right hand has done mighty things!" (Psalm 118:15, emphasis added)*

This scripture says that shouts of joy and victory resound in the tents of the righteous. If you believe in Jesus with your heart, You are righteous. You are made right with God. No matter what you have done previously, you are now righteous before your Heavenly Father. You are redeemed by the redemptive work of Christ on the cross.

Declarations: I am the righteousness of God in Christ Jesus. I am redeemed from all sorrow, sadness, grief, depression and all like things because of what Jesus did for me. I am made new. The old sinful man/ woman is dead and I am a new creation in Christ Jesus. The power of sin is broken in my life. It no longer has dominion over me. I am free from sin's power and effect in my life because of Jesus, who lives in me. I now have God's nature in me and His nature is joyful.

"Your statutes are my heritage forever; they are the
joy *of my heart" (Psalm 119:111, emphasis added).*

God's Word (Statues) brings joy to my heart. God's Word is my
inheritance from Him. As I read and think about God's Word and His
Promises to me, my mind is renewed and I am set free from bondages
and the lies of the enemy. It is the truth that sets me free.

Prayer: Father, thank You that all Your promises in the Bible are
my inheritance. Help me to know what these promises are so that I
may receive them, in Jesus' Name.

"When the Lord brought back the captives to Zion,
we were like men who dreamed. Our mouths were
filled with laughter, our tongues with songs of ***joy***.
Then it was said among the nations, "The Lord has
done great things for them". The Lord has done great
things for us and we are filled with ***joy***. *Restore our*
fortunes, O Lord, like streams in the Negev. Those
who sow in tears will reap with songs of ***joy***. *He who*
goes out weeping carrying seed to sow, will return
with songs of ***joy***, *carrying sheaves with him" (Psalm*
126, emphasis added).

Have you ever dreamed of good things coming your way? When
we experience the manifestation of our freedom from captivity and
bondage, it is like we are dreaming. We will laugh and sing joyful
songs. Our sorrow will be turned to joy.

The weeping in the above scripture reference represents our heartfelt prayers to the Lord. When we fervently pray and seek His face,
God hears our prayers and answers them and we are filled with joy. We
don't need to beg God for anything as He freely gives us all things. The
tears in this scripture are heartfelt prayers that are prayed from a place
of victory and not defeat. They are the prayers of a victor, not a beggar.

"May your priests be clothed with righteous-
ness; may your saints sing for ***joy***" *(Psalm 132:9,*
emphasis added).

As children of God, the Bible says we are no longer sinners but saints and priests of the Most High God.

Declarations: I am God's child. I am a priest and a saint in God's eyes and I am clothed with righteousness. I am clothed with Jesus Christ Himself. Therefore, I will sing for joy.

> *"Praise the Lord. Sing to the Lord a new song, his praise in the assembly of the saints. Let Israel rejoice in their Maker; let the people of Zion be glad in their King. Let them praise his name with dancing and make music to him with tambourine and harp. For the Lord takes delight in his people; he crowns the humble with salvation. Let the saints rejoice in this honor and sing for **joy** on their beds" (Psalm 149:1-5, emphasis added).*

It is a great honor to praise God and sing to Him. God wants you to rejoice in Him, be glad in Him, dance before Him and make music in your heart to Him. This is the will of God for you, His child. Why? Because He delights in seeing you happy and joyful.

> *"The prospect of the righteous is **joy**" (Proverbs 10:28a, emphasis added).*

Prospect means expectation or outlook. Joy is what you can expect from God. We need to come before the Lord with a heart of expectation. It pleases God to know that His children are expecting to receive from Him all that He has already provided through the redemptive work of Jesus. When Jesus said "It is finished" He was saying I have provided everything you need in this life. Now it is up to us to simply believe it and receive it by faith.

> *"There is deceit in the hearts of those who plot evil, but **joy** for those who promote peace" (Proverbs 12:20, emphasis added).*

Peacemakers will live in God's joy. Choose this day to be a peacemaker.

"A man finds joy in giving an apt reply and how good is a timely word. A cheerful look brings joy to the heart, and good news gives health to the bones" (Proverbs 15:23,30, emphasis added).

A smile, either given or received, brings joy. A kind word, either given or received, brings joy. Good news brings joy. God's Word is good news to you and to me and it brings joy.

"So I commend the enjoyment of life, because nothing is better for a man under the sun than to eat and drink and be glad. Then joy will accompany him in his work all the days of the life God has given him under the sun" (Ecclesiastes 8:15, emphasis added).

This was written by King Solomon to whom God had given much wisdom. He did a lot of soul searching in his lifetime and He realized that it is God's will for us to be glad in our every day living and to be joyful as we work unto the Lord. As we do this, burdens will be lifted off of our shoulders and we will experience the life that Jesus died to give us.

"You have enlarged the nation and increased their joy; they rejoice before you as people rejoice at the harvest, as men rejoice when dividing the plunder. For as in the day of Midian's defeat, you have shattered the yoke that burdens them, the bar across their shoulders, the rod of their oppressor" (Isaiah 9:3-4, emphasis added).

The harvest is a time when those who have sowed and planted are now reaping from their labors. This is not only a financial harvest but a harvest of everything we have planted. God's Word is alive and active. It brings life to us. Be careful what you plant. When we plant God's Word into our hearts, we will reap what we have planted.

Prayer: Father help me to sow and plant good things in my life and those I am praying for so that my harvest will be plentiful and bring me great joy. Thank You, Father, that the rod of my oppressor is shattered, in Jesus' Name!

Thank Him like you believe it.

*"Strengthen the feeble hands, steady the knees that give way; say to those with fearful hearts, "Be strong, do not fear; your God will come, he will come with vengeance; with divine retribution he will come to save you." Then will the eyes of the blind be opened and the ears of the deaf unstopped. Then will the lame leap like a deer, and the mute tongue shout for **joy**. Water will gush forth in the wilderness and streams in the desert. The burning sand will become a pool, the thirsty ground bubbling springs. In the haunts where jackals once lay, grass and reeds and papyrus will grow. And a highway will be there; it will be called the Way of Holiness. The unclean will not journey on it; it will be for those who walk in that Way; wicked fools will not go about on it. No lion will be there, nor will any ferocious beast get up on it; they will not be found there. But only the redeemed will walk there, and the ransomed of the Lord will return. They will enter Zion with singing; everlasting **joy** will crown their heads. Gladness and **joy** will overtake them, and sorrow and sighing will flee away" (Isaiah 35:3-10, emphasis added).*

This is a picture of a child of God receiving the blessings of his/her Heavenly Daddy. If we believe in Jesus with our hearts, we are on that highway that is called the Way of Holiness. The unbeliever (unclean) cannot walk on that highway. Only those who believe can walk on that highway. When we walk on that highway, God will bring us out of that dry and parched life into a life of joy, peace and righteousness in the Holy Spirit.

Put your focus on Jesus who is the **Way** and He will rescue and deliver you from everything that tries to destroy you.

Prayer: Father, in Jesus' Name, help me to focus on Jesus and who He is and not on myself or my circumstances.

> *"Let the desert and its towns raise their voices; let the settlements where Kedar lives **rejoice**. Let the people of Sela sing for **joy**; let them shout from the mountaintops. Let them give glory to the Lord and proclaim his praise in the islands. The Lord will march out like a mighty man, like a warrior he will stir up his zeal, with a shout he will raise the battle cry and will triumph over his enemies" (Isaiah 42:11-13, emphasis added).*

Jesus is our Commander in Chief. He is a mighty warrior, strong in battle and He triumphs every time. The battle is His and the victory is ours. He already defeated the enemy of our soul on the cross. We have the victory because of the finished work of Jesus Christ. As we seek His face and know that we are the righteousness of God in Christ Jesus we will triumph over our enemies in this lifetime.

> *"I have swept away your offenses like a cloud, your sins like the morning mist. Return to me, for I have redeemed you. Sing for **joy**, O heavens, for the Lord has done this; shout aloud, O earth beneath. Burst into song, you mountains, you forests and all your trees, for the Lord has redeemed Jacob, he displays his glory in Israel" (Isaiah 44:22-23, emphasis added).*

If you have slipped away from the Way of the Lord (doing your own thing), it is time to repent which means to turn back to Jesus and receive His grace. He has already forgiven you of your sins. Don't condemn yourself. Forgive yourself. Receive His forgiveness and turn to Him. He is waiting for you to come to Him so that you can experience all His goodness towards you. He loves you. Allow the joy of the Lord to return to you.

> *"This is what the Lord says – your Redeemer, the*
> *Holy One of Israel: "I am the Lord your God, who*
> *teaches you what is best for you, who directs you in*
> *the way you should go. Leave Babylon, flee from the*
> *Babylonians! Announce this with shouts of joy and*
> *proclaim it. Send it out to the ends of the earth; say,*
> *"The Lord has redeemed his servant Jacob" (Isaiah*
> *48:17,20, emphasis added).*

Is Jesus your Lord? If not, this is necessary for you to walk in victory. You can ask Jesus to be the Lord of your life. When you do this, He promises to teach you what is best for you and to direct you in the way you should go. If you have ventured into worldly things, repent and run back into God's arms of grace. He will help you get the victory and He will set you firmly upon a solid foundation where you will be protected when the storms come.

Prayer: Father, I ask that Jesus would be the Lord of my life. I repent of going my own way and doing my own thing. Lord, teach me what is best for me and direct me in the way I should go. Protect me in the storms and bring me safely through them to victory, in Jesus' Name.

> *"Shout for joy, O heavens; rejoice, O earth; burst*
> *into song, O mountains! For the Lord comforts his*
> *people and will have compassion on his afflicted*
> *ones" (Isaiah 49:13, emphasis added).*

Rejoice, shout, burst into song (put your name here). Tell yourself to praise God. David said in Psalm 103:1 "Praise the Lord O my soul; all my inmost being, praise his holy name". You can tell yourself to praise God just like David did. Praise the Lord O my soul. Praise the Lord Jeannette. Start thanking Jesus and praising His Holy Name for He is worthy of all our praise. Thank Him for all the good things in your life. Only dwell on the good things and thank Him.

> *"The Lord will surely comfort Zion and will look*
> *with compassion on all her ruins; he will make her*
> *deserts like Eden, her wastelands like the garden*

of the Lord. ***Joy*** *and gladness will be found in her,*
thanksgiving and the sound of singing" (Isaiah 51:3,
emphasis added).

Zion represents the place where God dwells. Since Jesus dwells
in all those who believe in Him, then we are "Zion". God promises
to comfort us (Zion). He says He will have compassion on us and
He will restore us and bring light and beauty into our darkness so
that joy, gladness, thanksgiving and singing will be our portion. Read
the promise again. Receive this promise. God is not a man that He
should lie to us. He speaks only that which is Truth. Think about how
beautiful the garden of Eden must have been. God says in this scripture that He will make our deserts like Eden, our wastelands like the
garden of the Lord. This makes me want to get up and dance for joy.

Prayer: Father, in Jesus' Name, thank You that You comfort me
and look on me with compassion. I receive Your comfort and compassion. You make my dry places beautiful and cause them to spring
to life just like the garden of Eden. Thank You that joy, gladness,
thanksgiving and singing are my portion.

"The ransomed of the Lord will return. They will enter
*Zion with singing; everlasting **joy** will crown their*
heads. Gladness and joy will overtake them, and
sorrow and sighing will flee away" (Isaiah 51:11,
emphasis added).

We are the ransomed of the Lord because Jesus has redeemed us.
When we become aware that Jesus redeemed us from sorrow, sadness,
etc., healing will arise within us and gladness and joy will overtake
us. This scripture says that sorrow and sighing will flee away from
us when we enter God's Presence with singing. Did you see that?

Sometimes it happens miraculously but most of the time it happens little by little, and over a period of time a big change takes place.

Declaration: I am redeemed from sorrow, grief, sadness and
all negative emotions by the blood of the Lamb and my emotions
are blessed.

Prayer: Father, in Jesus' Name, please bring me into Your Presence and help me to abide there.

"You will go out in joy and be led forth in peace; the mountains and hills will burst into song before you, and all the trees of the field will clap their hands" *(Isaiah 55:12, emphasis added).*

God always leads us in peace. If we don't have peace, we are not to proceed. We are to stay put and wait upon the Lord. We should always have peace first before we make final decisions. This is a safeguard from making wrong decisions and suffering the consequences of those decisions. Trust me I know. I have made some wrong financial decisions which cost me a lot and robbed me of joy.

If you have made wrong decisions, ask God for His grace in your mistakes. Hallelujah, there is grace in our mistakes.

Prayer: Father, in Jesus' Name, I ask for Your grace in my mistakes.

"And foreigners who bind themselves to the Lord to serve him, to love the name of the Lord and to worship him, all who keep the Sabbath without desecrating it and who hold fast to my covenant – these I will bring to my holy mountain and give them joy in my house of prayer" *(Isaiah 56:6-7a, emphasis added).*

God's holy mountain is a place where He dwells and it is a place of intimacy with our Father, Jesus and Holy Spirit. When we come into God's Presence, there is joy. When we fellowship with Him, there is joy. When we hear Him speak to us (even if it is correction), there is joy. When we serve Him, not out of duty but because we know He loves us and we love Him in return, there is joy. When we worship Him because we want to and not out of duty, there is joy. When we are intimate with Him, there is joy.

Tell the Lord how much you want intimacy with Him, how much you want to fellowship with Him. Tell Him that you want to know Him more and more. Prayer is simply talking to God. He will be the

Love of your life if you want Him to be. If you want this, go ahead and tell Him now.

God's Presence is so sweet. There is nothing that compares with it. The unsaved people in this world are looking for peace. They will get into a yoga position and chant to get peace. They will empty their minds so that they can find peace but what they are, in fact, doing is opening up their spirit to the demonic realm which will rob them of peace. They may find a temporary peace but nothing the devil brings lasts and he always has an ulterior motive. He is a counterfeit. God's peace is the real deal. It is part of the fruit of the Spirit which already resides in you. You need to know this so that you can draw on the peace of the Holy Spirit that is in you. Sit quietly before Him, focus on Him and receive His peace.

> *"If you keep your feet from breaking the Sabbath and from doing as you please on my holy day, if you call the Sabbath a delight and the Lord's holy day honorable, and if you honor it by not going your own way and not doing as you please or speaking idle words, then you will find your **joy** in the Lord, and I will cause you to ride on the heights of the land and to feast on the inheritance of your father Jacob." The mouth of the Lord has spoken"* (Isaiah 58:13-14, emphasis added).

Some are in the habit of doing their own thing and going their own way. They do not go to the house of the Lord to worship Him and to fellowship with other believers. God's Word says in Hebrews 10:25 that we are not to forsake meeting together with other believers. Why? The above scripture tells us that we will find joy in the Lord when we honor Jesus by meeting together with other believers and setting time aside to worship Him corporately. This is for our benefit.

Going to Church does not make you any more righteous than you already are. However, God knows we need Christian fellowship and wants us to be a functioning part of His Body. God has made each one of us a part of His Body. If we all go our own way and do our own thing, the Body is not united and is not functioning the way God intended it to. If the legs, arms, eyes, ears, feet, hands, etc. are all scattered about in different places, how can the Body of Christ function?

If you are not in a Church, you can pray and ask your Heavenly Father, in Jesus' Name, to direct you to the Church that is right for you. I come in agreement with you and ask God the Father, in Jesus' Name, to lead you to that right Church/fellowship where you can be loved, encouraged, built up in the Word of God, have fellowship with other members of the Body of Christ, grow up in your salvation now that you have tasted that the Lord is good and be a functioning part of the Body of Christ.

*"My servants will sing out of the **joy** of their hearts"*
(Isaiah 65:14a, emphasis added).

In the world, you don't normally hear anyone singing out of their depression, sorrow, sadness, discouragement, etc. God's Word says that His ways are higher than our ways. His ways are different than the world's ways. In order to come out from these things that are suppressing you, ask God to put a song in your heart. It will be a song that will deliver you from these things and replace them with joy. Psalm 32:7 says "You are my hiding place; you will protect me from trouble and surround me with **songs of deliverance**."

Prayer: Father, in Jesus' Name, please place a song in my heart that will deliver me from whatever is suppressing me and oppressing me and fill me with Your joy.

When a song arises in your heart, sing it. Even though you may not feel like singing, offer it as a sacrifice of praise unto the Lord. It will be a song that has words of encouragement for you and praise unto God.

God may lead you to purchase a particular Christian music CD that you need to listen to over and over again. I have purchased some CD's with songs that have ministered deep into my soul and that were exactly what I needed at that time. Some of these CD's I have listened to for a year or longer because they kept ministering to me over and over again. Ask God for the right Christian CD for you.

There is a song called "When Peace Like a River (It is well with my soul)". Google it and let the words of this song permeate your heart.

You can have praise and worship playing in your home continually. I even go to bed with a worship CD on in my bedroom. Even though I fall to sleep before the CD is finished, the worship is still going into my spirit while I am sleeping.

> *"When your words came, I ate them; they were my **joy** and my heart's delight, for I bear your name O Lord God almighty" (Jeremiah 15:16, emphasis added).*

You are to eat God's Word. In fact, the Bible says you can chew on the meat of the Word of God. This means to meditate on God's Word, to think about what God is speaking to you in His Word. Ponder it in your heart and speak it out loud. This causes God's Word to be planted firmly on the inside of you (your heart). It is food to your spirit and soul just like natural food is to your body. If you do not eat, your body will be sickly and weak. If you do not feed your spirit and soul with God's Word, your spirit and soul will be weak. God's Word is sustenance to your spirit and soul. It sustains you even in the storms of life.

> *"I will build you up again and you will be rebuilt, O virgin Israel. Again you will take up your tambourines and go out to dance with the **joyful**" (Jeremiah 31:4, emphasis added).*

The Lord was speaking to Israel in this scripture. We who have Jesus in our hearts are spiritual Israel today. He was telling Israel that although they had strayed from Him, He would forgive their sins and bring them back and that they would once again enjoy a close relationship with Him and they would be filled with joy. You may not have strayed from the Lord but, perhaps, the enemy has robbed you of the joy of your salvation. God wants to encourage you that He will build you up again and you will walk in the joy of the Lord.

> *"They will come and shout for **joy** on the heights of Zion; they will rejoice in the bounty of the Lord – the*

grain, the new wine and the oil, the young of the flocks and herds. They will be like a well-watered garden, and they will sorrow no more. The maidens will dance and be glad, young men and old as well. I will turn their mourning into gladness; I will give them comfort and joy instead of sorrow. I will satisfy the priests with abundance, and my people will be filled with my bounty," declares the Lord" (Jeremiah 31:12-14, emphasis added).

These are God's promises to us. Think about this. Jesus said in John 10:10 "The thief comes only to steal and kill and destroy, but I have come that they may have life and have it to the full." The above scripture talks about fullness of life (filled with my bounty).

Jesus defeated the thief (the devil) on the cross of Calvary for us through His death and resurrection. He took upon Himself all our negative emotions. He bore them for us so that we could be free from them. Jesus defeated mourning, sorrow, lack, depression, sadness, etc. that all come from the thief. Therefore, as God's child, the thief (whatever it is in our life that is robbing us of joy) is defeated in our life and we have fullness of life. Zoe life. The God kind of life. God is full of joy, love and peace. He lacks nothing. He radiates everything that represents good. As a child of God, this is our inheritance. Please accept it.

Prayer: Father, in Jesus' Name, I give You the ungodly emotions in my life. I now realize that You, Jesus, bore these things on the cross of Calvary for me. By Your grace, I refuse to bear them any longer. By Your grace, I refuse to allow the thief to rob me of what Jesus died to give me. I receive Your grace, righteousness, joy, peace, hope and gladness in abundance in my life. I thank You for Godly emotions and for turning my thinking right side up where it was upside down.

The thief brings sorrow, sadness, grief, etc. to rob you of peace, joy and righteousness in the Holy Spirit. The thief is not going to let go of you easily. He wants to destroy your life. However, remember that God in you is more powerful than the thief. There is no comparison. Thank your heavenly Daddy, in Jesus' Name, for Godly emotions, etc. Thank Him often. In the beginning you may need to thank

Him a lot, but eventually the Godly emotions will begin to arise in you. Persevere until the victory comes. Ask God to help you to persevere. When you ask God to help you, you are calling on His grace and not thinking that you can do it on your own. Remember that the battle is the Lord's and the victory is yours. Jesus has already fought the battle and He won! The enemy is defeated in your life already. Our battle is to fight the good fight of faith. Our battle is to continue to believe in Jesus and in His finished work for us. Our battle is to keep our eyes on Jesus in the storm. Our battle is not fought in our own power but in His mighty power! Our battle is being fought not from a place of defeat, but from a position of victory in Christ. Jesus has already gained the victory for you.

The Bible says you are seated with Jesus as a co-heir at the right hand of God the Father far above all rule and authority, power and dominion of the evil one. In other words, the thief is under your feet. Think about this. Think about your position in Christ Jesus.

Prophetic Act: Trample on the thief right now. Stand up and trample upon the sorrow, sadness, etc.

This is a prophetic act of your faith. By doing this you are saying that, as a child of God, the enemy is under your feet. You are saying that sorrow, sadness, etc. are under your feet. You are saying that Jesus is more powerful than the thief that brings these negative emotions. You are declaring to the enemy loud and clear that he is defeated in your life. Get up and trample upon him now. Please don't allow the enemy to continue to defeat you. Let him know by this prophetic act of faith that you have had enough and that he is under your feet.

Remember I said earlier in this book, that the curse of the law was nailed to the cross? Therefore, the curse is destroyed in your life and the blessings of God are flowing.

Declaration: I declare that the curse is destroyed over my emotions and my emotions are blessed in Jesus' mighty Name.

*"Yet I will rejoice in the Lord, I will be **joyful** in God my Savior" (Habakkuk 3:18, emphasis added).*

Habakkuk is expressing a strong faith in God in spite of unfavorable circumstances in his life. Joy is an expression of our faith in God, not an expression of our circumstances (whether they are good or not). We can choose to be joyful. You can make that choice now.

Declarations: I choose to be joyful. I choose to walk in the joy of the Lord. The joy of the Lord is my strength.

> *"The Ephramites will become like mighty men, and their hearts will be glad as with wine. Their children will see it and be **joyful**; their hearts will rejoice in the Lord" (Zechariah 10:7, emphasis added).*

When God empowers us and strengthens us our hearts become joyful. Our children are encouraged by our joy and they too become joyful.

Prayer: Father, in Jesus' Name, thank You for strengthening my heart and for encouraging me daily for You are my joy. You are my God in whom I put my trust.

> *"The kingdom of heaven is like treasure hidden in a field. When a man found it he hid it again, and then in his **joy** went and sold all he had and bought that field" (Matthew 13:44, emphasis added).*

This scripture is talking about the kingdom of heaven. The treasure is Jesus. The price the man paid was his life. He joyfully gave his life to Jesus and Jesus gave him Himself and the Kingdom of heaven. There is no greater treasure than this.

> *"The angel said to the women, "Do not be afraid, for I know that you are looking for Jesus, who was crucified. He is not here, he is risen, just as he said. Come and see the place where he lay. Then go quickly and tell his disciples: He has risen from the dead and is going ahead of you into Galilee. There you will see him. Now I have told you." So the women hurried away from the tomb, afraid yet filled with*

joy, and ran to tell his disciples" (Matthew 28:5-8, emphasis added).

The women were afraid yet at the same time they were filled with joy that Jesus had risen from the dead and that they were going to see Him again in Galilee. News about Jesus brings joy to our hearts. Although we cannot see Him, He is with us always. We need to think about this. Jesus lives in our hearts. Imagine that! God Himself living in us. He is as close as the mention of His Name.

Prophetic Act: Close your eyes and say his Name. Jesus! Jesus! Jesus!

Something begins to stir on the inside of us when we call out His Name.

"When it was time for Elizabeth to have her baby, she gave birth to a son. Her neighbors and relatives heard that the Lord had shown her great mercy, and they shared her joy" (Luke 1:57-58, emphasis added).

Good news brings joy. Also, God's mercy brings joy. Enough joy that it can be shared with others.

Prayer: Father, in Jesus' Name, I thank You that You show me mercy. Your Word says that Your mercies are new every morning. I pray that You will remind me of this so that I will receive Your mercies every morning for each day.

"But the angel said to them, "Do not be afraid. I bring you good news of great joy that will be for all the people" (Luke 2:10, emphasis added).

The news was that a Savior had been born and He is Christ the Lord. Jesus came to save all the people and to fill all with joy. That includes you and me.

Declaration: Thank You Jesus that I am filled with Your joy. You are my joy and my heart's delight.

*"Blessed are you when men hate you, when they exclude you and insult you and reject your name as evil, because of the Son of Man. Rejoice in that day and leap for **joy**, because great is your reward in heaven. For that is how their fathers treated the prophets" (Luke 6:22-23, emphasis added).*

God says that, as His child, we can have joy even when we are rejected, persecuted and mistreated by man because of our faith in His Son, Jesus. He tells us to rejoice and leap for joy. Will you do this? I'm saying "Will you do this"?

Prophetic Act: Stand on your feet and leap for joy.

As you stand to your feet and leap for joy make the following declarations.

Declarations: I declare that I am the head and not the tail, I am the top and not the bottom. I declare that rejection, persecution, depression, discouragement, sorrow, sadness, etc. are under my feet. I have the victory in Jesus Christ.

*"The seventy-two returned with **joy** and said, "Lord, even the demons submit to us in your name" (Luke 10:17, emphasis added).*

It brought joy to the 72 when they took authority over demons and people were set free. It also brought joy to them when they experienced the power of God in using the Name of Jesus. We need to understand just how powerful the Name of Jesus is. Always pray and take authority in the Name of Jesus.

*"However, do not rejoice that the spirits submit to you, but rejoice that your names are written in heaven." At that time, Jesus, full of **joy** through the Holy Spirit, said, "I praise you, Father, Lord of heaven and earth, because you have hidden these things from the wise and learned, and revealed them to little children. Yes, Father, for this was your good pleasure" (Luke 10:20-21, emphasis added).*

Jesus was full of joy because the 72 saw demons flee in His Name. They reported to Jesus how people were set free in His Name. God enjoys seeing His children being set free from bondages and full of joy. He takes delight in it and He is blessed by it.

Do you see the power in the Name of Jesus? The disciples were able to cast demons out of people in the Name of Jesus. Because of the powerful Name of Jesus people were set free from demons and bondages that held them captive. The Bible says in Philippians 2:10-11 that at the Name of Jesus every knee should bow, in heaven and on earth and under the earth, and every tongue confess that Jesus Christ is Lord to the glory of God the Father. Therefore, every demon, every wrong emotion, etc. must bow to the Name of Jesus. As a child of God, you can command sorrow, grief, sadness, depression and every like thing to leave you, in the Name of Jesus, and go where Jesus is telling them to go. When you do this cover yourself, those around you and your family with the precious blood of Jesus. Jesus died on the cross and shed His blood for you. The blood of Jesus protects you.

Prayer: Heavenly Father, in the Name of Jesus, I cover myself, my family and those around me with the precious blood of Jesus. I thank You, Jesus, for shedding Your blood for us and for Your protection. In the Name of Jesus, I command all sorrow, grief, sadness, depression, despair, hopelessness, oppression, death and every like think that would rob me of joy and the life that Jesus died to give me to leave me now and go where Jesus is telling you to go. I forbid you to transfer to anyone else. Thank You, Father, in Jesus' Name that I am free because of the finished work of Jesus Christ on the cross of Calvary. Father, I ask that You would please fill me with Your peace, joy and righteousness of the Holy Spirit so that there will never be any place for these ungodly emotions to return to me. Please seal me in Your precious Holy Spirit, in Jesus' Name I pray.

> *"When he had said this, he showed them his hands and feet. And while they still did not believe it because of **joy** and amazement, he asked them, "Do you have anything to eat" (Luke 24:40-41, emphasis added).*

Jesus appeared to some of His disciples after He was raised from the dead and they were filled with joy. They thought He was dead and now they realized He was alive and He was standing in their midst.

> *"To this John replied, "A man can receive only what is given him from heaven. You yourselves can testify that I said, "I am not the Christ but am sent ahead of him." The bride belongs to the Bridegroom. The friend who attends the Bridegroom waits and listens for him, and is full of joy when he hears the Bridegroom's voice. That joy is mine and it is now complete. He must become greater; I must become less" (John 3:27-30, emphasis added).*

John was referring to himself when he talked about the "friend" attending the Bridegroom. The Bridegroom is referring to Jesus. John was expecting the Bridegroom to come and he was waiting and listening for Him. When he heard the Bridegroom's voice, he was filled with joy. I, too, am to wait & listen for the voice of my Bridegroom and when I hear Him I, too, will be filled with joy. Jesus says in John 10:4 that we are His sheep and that His sheep hear His voice. Therefore, I can hear the voice of my Bridegroom, Jesus. It is a voice that comes from the inside of me where Jesus dwells because I have asked Him to live in my heart. It is not a voice that comes from the outside of me.

When God speaks, whatever He says will always line up with the Word of God. He never contradicts Himself. When God speaks, He will lead us forth in peace. There will not be fear when God speaks to us. God never brings shame or condemnation when He speaks to us. He will bring life, encouragement, direction and freedom. However, there are times when God will discipline us if we are going the wrong way (because He loves us) so that we will come back under His grace and back into that place of victory but it is always with love (never condemnation).

Prayer: Father, in Jesus' Name, please help me to hear Your voice and to do what You are calling me to do.

*"I tell you the truth, you will weep and mourn while the world rejoices. You will grieve, but your grief will turn to **joy**" (John 16:20).*

Jesus knew that He was going to die on the cross but the disciples did not know this at that time. The world rejoiced at Jesus' death but His disciples mourned His death. Jesus also knew that He would rise from the grave, that the disciples would see Him again and that they would rejoice in His resurrection. Because we believe in Jesus' resurrection and that one day we will be with Him for all eternity, we are filled with joy. In fact, we are already with Him as He lives in us and we in Him.

*"A Woman giving birth to a child has pain because her time has come; but when her baby is born she forgets the anguish because of her joy that a child is born into the world. So with you: Now is your time of grief, but I will see you again and you will rejoice and no one will take away your joy. In that day you will no longer ask me anything. I tell you the truth, my Father will give you whatever you ask in my name. Until now you have not asked for anything in my name. Ask and you will receive, and your **joy** will be complete" (John 16:21-24, emphasis added).*

Jesus continues to talk here about His death and resurrection and then He begins to teach them about prayer. Up until His death, the disciples were with Jesus and He provided everything they needed. He goes on to say "In that day" referring to when He is no longer in human form. He proceeds to talk to them about prayer and intercession. He says "In that day you will no longer **ask me** anything. I tell you the truth, **my Father** will give you whatever you **ask in my name**. Until now you have not asked for anything in my name. Ask and you will receive, and your joy will be complete." He is telling the disciples how to get their needs met "in that day". He tells them to ask their Heavenly Father, in Jesus' Name, for what they need. When we use the Name of Jesus, it is as if Jesus Himself is asking His Father on our behalf. The Father will not deny Jesus. He will not deny us when we use Jesus' Name. He is telling them that when they ask in His Name, they will receive and their joy will be complete. Prayer and Intercession can be painful like child birth. As we stand by faith on God's Word for His promises for ourselves and as we stand in the gap for someone in need, it can be painful while we wait but when the answer comes the pain is forgotten and is replaced with joy and no one will be able to take that joy away. When we pray for ourselves and when we stand on God's promises and intercede for others, we will receive answers to our prayers and our joy will be complete. However, all our asking should be in accordance with God's Word.

"And the disciples were filled with joy and with the Holy Spirit" (Acts 13:52, emphasis added).

The disciples were filled with joy and with the Holy Spirit because the Gospel was now being brought to the Gentiles (verses 46-47), because the whole city gathered to hear the Word of God (verse 44) and the Word of God spread through the whole region. Many believed in Jesus and were saved. This brought great joy to the disciples as they experienced the Holy Spirit moving powerfully through them. God was using the disciples to reach the lost for His Kingdom and to bring the lost into the fullness of what God had for them. God will use you too. You may not be an apostle or a pastor but God will use you in the way that He has gifted you. You are an important part in the Body of Christ. Without you, the Body is lacking.

"Yet he has not left himself without testimony: He has shown kindness by giving you rain from heaven and crops in their seasons; he provides you with plenty of food and fills your hearts with joy" (Acts 14:17, emphasis added).

God is a generous Giver. He is not stingy. He is the God of more than enough. Just as He sent rain to water the crops so that they would grow, He blesses the work of our hands and brings forth His abundant provision at His perfect timing. He fills our hearts with joy as we experience His provision and Presence in our lives. Joy comes to us as we know and experience that God cares about our every need and abundantly provides for us.

In Ephesians 3:20 God says that He does immeasurably, exceedingly, abundantly above and beyond all that we could ever ask, imagine or think according to His great power that is at work within us.

Prayer: Thank You, Father, in Jesus' Name, that You do immeasurably, exceedingly, abundantly above and beyond all that I could ever ask, imagine or think according to Your great power that is at work within me.

God is generous in every area of our lives (not just our finances). God wants us to prosper in every area of our lives i.e. our emotions, our relationships, our health, etc.

> *"May the God of hope fill me with all **joy** and peace as I trust in him, so that I may overflow with hope by the power of the Holy Spirit" (Romans 15:13, emphasis added).*

As I put my trust in the Lord, He will fill me with joy and peace and my heart will overflow with hope. God is a God of abundance. He gives us enough joy that it will overflow so that others will also be affected.

Prayer: Father, in Jesus' Name, I put my trust in You alone. You are the God of hope. Thank You that my heart is overflowing with hope by the power of Your Spirit. Thank You that I am filled to overflowing with Your joy and Your peace, in Jesus' Name.

> *"And now, brothers, we want you to know about the grace that God has given the Macedonian churches. Out of the most severe trial, their **overflowing joy** and their extreme poverty welled up in rich generosity" (2 Corinthians 8:1-2, emphasis added).*

Amidst my extreme trials and poverty, because of God's grace to me, I can have overflowing joy and I can be liberal in my generosity as God directs me to give. I am to give what God directs me to give with joy and out of love for Him, not out of duty and not begrudg-ingly. Ask God what you are to give. Be led by His Spirit. God always leads us with His peace. The Bible says that we will reap what we sow. If I sow generously as the Holy Spirit directs me, I will reap generously. This does not mean it will be instantaneous, although sometimes that is true. Most of the time we sow into the Kingdom of God just like a farmer plants seeds into the ground. Day and night the farmer **expects** that seed to grow and patiently waits for the harvest. It is the same with us. We sow into the Kingdom of God (finances, love, time, etc.) and day and night we expect that seed to grow and we wait for the harvest. At the appointed time, when the harvest comes, we will reap what we have sown and we will overflow with joy.

This is also true with the Word of God. As we sow the Word of God into our hearts and continue to do so, we will reap a harvest from what we have sown. We will find that the Word of God is coming out of our mouth because it has been sown into our hearts. You have been sowing seeds of joy into your heart by reading this Book and you will reap a harvest from what you have sown. Your harvest is JOY.

> *"But the fruit of the Spirit is love, joy, peace, patience, kindness, goodness, faithfulness" (Galatians 5:22, emphasis added).*

Although you have joy on the inside of you already because the Holy Spirit lives in you, you need to be aware of this so that you can stir it up and draw upon that joy. When you stir up the joy of the Holy Spirit, it will become active in you. That's exactly what you have been doing by reading this Book and doing the prophetic acts of faith that I asked you to do. You have stirred up the joy of the Holy Spirit that is resident within you as you clapped your hands, shouted for joy and jumped in praise to God. You did it by faith in God. Joy is stirred up and becoming active inside of you. This is what God's Word does. God's Word is alive and active and it brings us the victory.

> *"You became imitators of us and of the Lord; in spite of severe suffering, you welcomed the message with*

the joy given by the Holy Spirit" (1 Thessalonians 1:6, emphasis added).

Even in times of severe suffering you can have joy as you stir it up. As you walk in the Spirit, nothing will be able to put out the fire of joy within you. Joy will overcome the negativity in your life. It will overcome the wrong thoughts that the enemy tries to bombard you with.

When the enemy is pressing in and attacking you, start to laugh out loud. Laugh in the face of the enemy. I do this sometimes. Of course, I'm by myself when I do it. By doing this you are declaring that the enemy is defeated and you are stirring up the joy of the Lord within you. Psalm 2:1-4 shows God laughing at His enemies. Why don't you do that right now.

Prophetic Act: Laugh out loud in the face of the enemy.

You can watch good clean shows that will make you laugh. I like to watch Funniest Home Videos as it makes me laugh.

"Be joyful always, pray continually, give thanks in all circumstances, for this is God's will for you in Christ Jesus" (1 Thessalonians 5:16-18, emphasis added).

It is God's will for you to be thankful and to be filled to overflowing with His joy. God wants to put a smile on your face. Jesus came to set you free from everything that would rob you of that smile.

Praying continually means to have a God consciousness (bringing God into your everyday living). You can be talking to God about simple things i.e. what to make for supper or what to do in a certain circumstance that you find yourself in.

"In all my prayers for all of you, I always pray with joy" (Philippians 1:4, emphasis added).

Paul prayed with joy because he prayed **with expectation.** We can know that when we pray in accordance with God's Word, He hears us. We can have joy that our prayers are answered even while we are waiting for the manifestation of our prayers.

"Welcome him in the Lord with great joy and honor
men like him, because he almost died for the work of
Christ, risking his life to make up for the help you could
not give me" (Philippians 2:29-30, emphasis added).

With great joy I am to welcome and honor people who have surrendered completely to the work of Christ even to the point of dying themselves. We are to honor men and women of God who have laid down their lives for the furtherance of the Gospel. We are to honor our Pastors for they look out for our best interests.

"For what is our hope, our joy or the crown in which
we will glory in the presence of our Lord Jesus when
he comes? Is it not you? Indeed, you are our glory
and joy" (1 Thessalonians 2:19-20, emphasis added).

Paul, a Minister of the Gospel of Jesus Christ, laid down his life to be obedient to the call of God. He says that his Ministry brings joy to him because he is doing what God called him to do and because of the lives that he is seeing changed. There is great reward in this life time and for all eternity when we lay down our lives to serve the Lord in what He has called us to do. It was not a burden to Paul but a delight. God has given each one of us gifts to serve Him in a specific way. Do you know what your gifts are that God has given to you? What desire has God placed on your heart to do for Him? You will find joy in answering the call of God. You may not be called to be a Pastor or an Evangelist but whatever it is that God has called you to do is equally important. The Body of Christ cannot function right or fully without you. As you experience God touching lives through you, you will have joy.

Prayer: Father, in Jesus' Name, please reveal to me what you have called me to do.

"You have loved righteousness and hated wickedness;
therefore God, your God, has set you above your
companions by anointing you with the oil of joy"
(Hebrews 1:9, emphasis added).

This scripture is talking about Jesus. Jesus has been anointed with the oil of joy. John 15:5 says that Jesus is in me and I am in Him. I am part of His Body. Romans 8:17 says that I am a co-heir with Jesus. All that belongs to Jesus is mine. God anointed Jesus with His joy and He anoints me with His joy as well. Think about that!

Declaration: I am anointed with the oil of joy just like Jesus.

*"Let us fix our eyes on Jesus, the author and perfecter of our faith, who for the **joy set before him** endured the cross, scorning its shame and sat down at the right hand of the throne of God" (Hebrews 12:2, emphasis added).*

Let us follow Jesus' example who fixed His eyes on the **joy** that would be His when He sat in His place of triumph. He looked not at the trial or the suffering, but rather at the **joy** of being victorious and saving many from the grasp of satan. He considered this trial as joy because He was looking at the end result (you and me being set free). **He saw, through the eyes of faith**, His reward (which was us) and this brought Him joy and this joy was His strength to endure the trial. **He saw** Himself sitting at the right hand of the throne of God (with us sitting there with Him) far above all rule and authority, power and dominion. **He saw** lost souls (sinners) being saved. **He saw** people in bondage being freed. **He saw** people being healed, delivered and made whole. **He saw** people being provided for and comforted and this brought enough joy to Jesus to give Him the strength He needed on the cross.

Prayer: Father, in Jesus' Name, please help me to fix my eyes on Jesus so that I may have joy and strength to endure the hardship until the victory comes.

*"Consider it pure **joy**, my brothers, whenever you face trials of many kinds, because you know that the testing of your faith develops perseverance. Perseverance must finish its work so that you may be mature and complete, not lacking anything" (James 1:2-4, emphasis added).*

I am not to quit and give up when I am in a trial. As I persevere **with His power** in the trial, I will become mature and complete and I will get the victory. It is always God's Will for us to be victorious. Knowing this brings joy and joy brings me strength to keep enduring until the victory comes.

Prayer: Father please help me to understand the things I need to know so that I will be encouraged to continue to fight the good fight of faith and to do what You are calling me to do with joy, in Jesus' Name.

I began this Book and I am ending this Book with Isaiah 61:1-3a, and Isaiah 61:7. Jesus really wants you to grab hold of the truth that He came to set you free.

> *"The Spirit of the Sovereign Lord is on me, because the Lord has anointed me to preach the good news to the poor. He has sent me to bind up the broken-hearted, to proclaim freedom for the captives and release from darkness for the prisoners, to proclaim the year of the Lord's favor and the day of vengeance of our God, to comfort all who mourn, and provide for those who grieve in Zion – to bestow on them a crown of beauty instead of ashes, **the oil of gladness instead of mourning**, and **a garment of praise instead of a spirit of despair**." (Isaiah 61:1-3a, emphasis added).*

The above scripture is referring to Jesus. Jesus was anointed by the Spirit of the Sovereign Lord. He came to earth as a man but God anointed Him to do all of the above so that people could be set free. Jesus came to give us gladness and joy which will deliver us from mourning, grieving, and sorrow. He came to give us a garment of praise which will deliver us from despair, hopelessness, depression and death. We need to receive what He died to give us. Will you receive it now?

> *"Instead of their shame my people will receive a double portion, and instead of disgrace, they will rejoice in their inheritance. And so they will inherit*

a double portion in their land, and everlasting joy
will be theirs" (Isaiah 61:7, emphasis added).

This is what Jesus came to give us. He came to remove shame and disgrace from His people and to bless us with a double portion of all that is good.

Will you receive a double portion of all that is good from the Lord Jesus Christ? Will you receive it right now for it is being offered to you free of charge. God only asks for your heart to believe in Him because that is where the victory is and He wants you to live a victorious life, a life full of joy, peace and all that is good.

Prayer: Father, in Jesus' Name, I receive the abundant life that Jesus died to give me. I receive a double portion of Your joy. I receive a double portion of Your Spirit so that I can praise You, my God. I receive a double portion of Your peace. I receive a double portion of hope. Jesus You are my Hope. I receive a double portion of Your comfort. I receive a double portion of Your encouragement. I receive a double portion of Your provision. I receive a double portion of Your help. I receive a double portion of Your healing. I receive a double portion of Your protection. I receive a double portion of Your strength. I receive a double portion of Your grace. Thank You Jesus for all that You did for me and for setting me free from captivity and bringing me into victory and wholeness.

I pray that you will walk in the freedom that Jesus came to give to you and that you will experience everlasting joy all the days of your life.

CPSIA information can be obtained
at www.ICGtesting.com
Printed in the USA
LVOW10s0904220317
528005LV00004B/9/P